THE ITALIAN COMMEDIA
AND
PLEASE BE GENTLE

Mask: A Release of Acting Resources

A series of books written and illustrated by David Griffiths

Volume 1
Acting through Mask
Written and illustrated by David Griffiths

Volume 2
The Training of Noh Actors and *The Dove*
Written and illustrated by David Griffiths

Volume 3
The Italian Commedia and *Please Be Gentle*
Written and illustrated by David Griffiths

Volume 4
The Masquerades of Nigeria and *Touch*
Written and illustrated by David Griffiths

This book is part of a series. The publisher will accept continuation orders which may be cancelled at any time and which provide for automatic billing and shipping of each title in the series upon publication. Please write for details.

THE ITALIAN COMMEDIA
AND
PLEASE BE GENTLE

Written and illustrated
by
David Griffiths

Routledge
Taylor & Francis Group

LONDON AND NEW YORK

Reprinted 2004
By Routledge
11 New Fetter Lane, London EC4P 4EE

Transferred to Digital Printing 2004

British Library Cataloguing in Publication Data

Griffiths, David
   The Italian commedia; and, Please be gentle.
   – (Mask: a release of acting resources; v. 3)
   1. Commedia dell'arte   2. Masques
   I. Title
   792. 2'3'028

   ISBN 3-7186-5717-1 (HB)
   ISBN 3-7186-5718-X (PB)

Applications for permission to perform *Please be Gentle* should be addressed to David Griffiths, Quaker Cottage, Quakers Lane, Rawdon, Leeds, LS19 6HU, England.

Cover illustrations by David Griffiths.

Printed and bound by Antony Rowe Ltd, Eastbourne

I dedicate this book to my late parents Jack and Doris,
who initiated and inspired the opportunity,
and to Vicky who supported me unselfishly throughout the period of
research and writing, and shared the joy of its completion.

CONTENTS

INTRODUCTION TO THE SERIES

Mask: A Release of Acting Resources is a fully illustrated four-volume series, which examines the effect of mask in performance.

This series reflects my practical work and draws upon my research into the secret world of the Noh of Japan and the Masquerade of Nigeria, the comic style of the Commedia Dell'Arte and the training of actors through mask in Britain.

The series also includes my three written masked plays called *The Dove*, *Please Be Gentle* and *Touch*, which transform and test the results of my experiments into theatrical practicality.

David Griffiths

ACKNOWLEDGEMENTS

I would like to thank the following: Dr David Richards for sowing the seed and making the original research enquiry on my behalf; the School of English, University of Leeds, for giving me the opportunity; the British Academy for setting the precedent of offering me an annual award and having faith that it would be used responsibly; Tom Needham for his friendship and his "investment" of £1000, without which I would not have been able to visit Japan; the Society of Friends for their grant of £500, which was given to me at a time great financial need; all those at the Tramshed in Glasgow who led me to *The Mahabharata* and Peter Brook; Chris and Vayu Banfield who have embraced me with a continuous stream of encouragement, practical help and invaluable advice; Alan Vaughan Williams, a wonderfully exciting theatre director, who gave me some of my early directing work and who continues to support and encourage without qualification; and Professor Martin Banham who supervised and guided me through my original enquiry with extreme care, the right amount of humour and encouraging portions of excitement.

In Japan, I am eternally grateful for the extraordinary hospitality and kindness given to me by my supervisor Professor Yasunari Takahashi, Jo Barnett CBE (Director of the British Council, Tokyo) and his staff at Kyoto, Chizuko and Naoichi Tsuyama my hosts and dear friends, Richard Emmert, and Fumiye Miho and Friends at the Friends' House in Tokyo.

LIST OF ILLUSTRATIONS

INTRODUCTION

It is no coincidence that this book on Commedia follows quite naturally from Volume 2 on Noh. Their position at the heart of the philosophical and practical arguments on actor-training are fundamentally juxtaposed and complementary.

One of the most exciting aspects of my early research into Noh and Commedia is the discovery of a number of familiar factors which emerged concerning the acting skills demanded by the two genres. At first glance, the frenetic comic elements of slapstick Commedia seemed to be on the diametrically opposite side of the theatrical spectrum to the slow, floating grace which characterises the Noh.

As I was casually making a series of charts tracing the development of the Commedia from its origins to its high Renaissance in the 16th Century, it was quite by chance that I discovered there were many familiar aspects common to Noh.

The problem with my (or any) investigation of Commedia, is one of establishing irrefutable facts. Understanding Commedia arises from careful conjecture and detailed reconstruction. Evidence in the form of extant scenarios, drawings, paintings and prints, and the Commedia influence contained in many of the works of playwrights from Shakespeare to Molière, has been the main source of now familiar documentation to which academics and theatre historians have referred.

All 'living' twentieth-century productions of Commedia by professional troupes such as the Co-Op Tag Teatro of Venice have been devised and reconstructed from the same resource material the only difference being one of direct and indirect access to letters, scenarios, and other documentation, through translation.

The last Commedia 'family' in the Noh sense died out at the end of the seventeenth century, and to a large extent took all the concrete evidence of their lifestyle and their training methods with them. One assumes that their 'vagabond' status was enough to make them and their theatre unworthy of documentation within the self-elevating circles of the literate.

In sharp contrast to this conjectural view – as we saw in the previous volume – the legacy of Noh still lives on in an uninterrupted flow of fact. The extant costumes, properties, masks and the guarded training and commitment of actors within the Noh families, contribute to a direct, much supported, present-day link, which can be traced accurately back through the centuries to its beginnings. Professional Noh continues to strive for the same sense of novelty prescribed by Zeami.

However, there is enough agreement between various authorities to be able to assume with reasonable accuracy the manner in which the Commedia Troupes evolved, the skills they required to learn and maintain in order to perform their singularly complex, comic theatre, and the manner in which they preserved their professional credibility and influence upon the other theatre developments in Europe.

So what, in general, are the common factors?

Firstly, the main characters in Noh and Commedia are familiar to their audience and masked. In Commedia, only the female characters are unmasked, although there are engravings and paintings by artists like Callot and Magiotto, who indicate clearly that small loup masks were sometimes used by women as part of the fashion of facial adornment. (See illustration 15)

As with Noh, the characters introduce themselves through their masks and their costumes. They are instantly recognisable. Who and what they represent are seen before they are heard.

Such was the design of the masks that the total psyche of each character was embodied within it. The mask *is* the character and all that follows in terms of a physical representation comes from it.

Similarly, there is no 'star' system where the actor and his reputation interferes with the character of the mask in the mind of the audience. The only 'stars' are the masks. Thus we have the same sense of humility encountered with the Noh; the actor submitting the whole of his energies and skills to the mask.

Secondly, the Commedia troupes travelled to their place of performance; only very rarely did they have a semi-permanent residential base owned and maintained by a wealthy patron. Their acting arena therefore was essentially temporary and fit-up, consisting of minimal properties and scenery, which allowed for the many displays of gymnastics and tumbling in a simple uncluttered space. It also placed a great emphasis and responsibility upon the visual skills of the actors. Their characters alone were the primary focus.

Thirdly, there is much documentation which indicates generations of actors preserving a tight sense of 'family' where the skills and the theatrical persona of well-known characters were handed down from one generation to the next, usually from father to son.

Fourthly, it is inevitable – given the degree of skill needed to work the mask in performance – that the Commedia actor like his Noh counterpart was endowed with many performing skills which required an extremely sharp mind to cope with the speed of thought and 'improvised' delivery, and also the physical agility to create the 'slapstick' comedy.

Fifthly, the Commedia actor was professional, in that his income, usually paid 'in kind', was determined by the quality and popularity of his performance; his livelihood and patronage depended upon this.

Finally the general tenor and style of his performance depended upon his close contact with and knowledge of his audience. He had to have that basic awareness and instinct for the mood and composition of his audience, and possess the wit and skills necessary to win and embrace their favour.

It could be argued that some of these factors are prerequisites of theatrical performances by all actors and not peculiar to those of Noh and Commedia. I don't dispute this. It is the way the actor is trained which is my main concern.

We are more familiar with the Commedia form in the West. In the last twenty years there has been a significant increase in performance and enquiry about the Commedia style and tradition. It is not therefore my intention to elaborate upon the dramatic form of the Commedia in the same detail as the Noh. On the following pages, I shall give a concise description of its evolution and development, the stage space, the content and structure of the extant scenarios, the style and colour coding of the costumes and properties, and the skills and training needed to present and sustain a Commedia performance.

All this is then exemplified in the form of a play, *Please Be Gentle*, which I describe as a modern masked commedia. It seemed to me that presenting all my ideas on the Commedia form in this way would help to clarify the practical details involved with the presentation and development of a traditional scenario.

Please Be Gentle is included for academic study and also to encourage practical experiment. There are many lazzi to play with, and many spaces for alternative lazzi to be included. On page 27 of this book I include my notes made during the rehearsal process with the original cast.

Ancient Greece to Molière

Based upon the extant evidence which we have before us, it would seem that the comic style of the Commedia Dell'Arte is dependent upon the special ability of its actors to display their agility with words and gymnastics; a combination of wit, satire and buffoonery.

I am in complete agreement with Allardyce Nicoll when he interprets the meaning of Commedia Dell'Arte as being 'the comedy of skill'. The very heart of my enquiry into the Commedia persuades me that the professional Commedia actor was as skillful as the Shite is in Noh.

In my view, one of the most important aspects of the comic performance in the Commedia relied upon the fact that the actors were masked.

3

The technical demands of performing in mask add another dimension to the same, perennial, comic devices and skills. It is my contention that the special and lasting quality of the theatrical traditions of farce, which survived over a thousand years of history, and consolidated its more familiar form in the Commedia Dell'Arte, was due to the continuing use of the mask by succeeding generations of actors.

It was the stock characters tested and tried and animated in their masks which sustained support rather than the generations of actors who played them. The masks were instantly recognisable personalities of the characters of life in any European landscape, in any community.

Greek and Roman actors were masked. This much we know. So the first legacy from Classical antecedents which the Commedia actors inherited was the mask. From this point onwards, finding similar derivation based upon solid fact is more difficult.

Whilst there is little concrete evidence to support the view that the origins of the Commedia were based in Classical theatre, there is an instinctive rationale which leads us to assume that this basic, comic, performing tradition, filtered directly or indirectly from the theatrical traditions of Greece and Rome.

There are three areas of popular – though not conclusive – theories of source material: namely, the *Satyr Dramas*, the *Phlyax Dramas* and the *Fabula Atellana Farce*.

The *Satyr Drama* was one of the prerequisites of repertoire of the Greek tragic poet. In presenting four plays at any performance, three of which were tragedies, the remaining play was a satyr play, the characteristics of which according to H.D.F. Kitto contained...

'rude action, vigorous dancing, boisterous fun, and indecency in speech and gesture'.[1]

It was as though the fundamental profoundness and seriousness of the tragedies was turned on its head and countered in burlesque, designed one assumes to provide a necessary release of tension of the audience through laughter, providing emotional respite and mental refreshment... This Yin and Yan balancing act echoes the Kyogen play set as it is in between the plays in a Noh cycle.

Much of what is known of the classical *Phlyax* mime-play is derived from over a hundred and fifty vase paintings found in southern Italy and is dated between 400–300 B.C.

The paintings depict masked characters, grotesquely padded and costumed, often displaying a phallus, and arranged in a wide variety of exaggerated comic gesture and situation.

---

[1] Hartnoll, P. *Oxford Companion to the Theatre* (Third Edition. Oxford, 1967) p. 838

The narratives and their characters are familiar, and are repeated in a number of wildly distorted versions of their tragic originals. According to Phyllis Hartnoll they included in their repertory many stock situations taken from 'plays based on the amorous adventures of Zeus and the Seven Labours of Hercules'.[2]

There are scenes of drunken debauchery and the traditional preoccupation with excesses of food, sex, and the stealing and gorging of both. Old men are dragged, pushed, and ridiculed, whilst women are fought over and abused. All of these scenes have been examined and catalogued by W. Beare in his book *The Roman Stage*, and so I don't propose to reproduce that evidence here, but of the paintings I have chosen to exemplify my theories, I shall dwell a moment to consider the staging depicted.

Even a casual glance at these paintings will clearly identify a raised, acting space which was simply designed and built, using a mainly fit-up, cloth-and-frame structure which hints of a temporary 'travelling' booth design associated with the Commedia tradition.

In the illustration 1a, Jupiter mounts a ladder to his lady love, whilst Mercury stands by with a torch and a decorated basket; in illustration 1b the same characters anticipate a similar activity, although the fact that the ladder is draped about the head of Jupiter, anticipates any amount of

1(a). 4th-century Phylax vase painting, British Museum, London

[2] Hartnoll, P. *A Concise History of the Theatre* (Thames and Hudson, 1968) p. 28

1(b). 4th-century Phylax vase painting, Vatican Museum, Rome

comic business to secure its removal. Perhaps Mercury will climb the ladder instead with Jupiter still imprisoned?

In illustration 1c an old miser Charinus is trying to protect his treasure chest from thieves, whilst in illustration 1d an old man Chiron is being pushed and pulled upstairs. In illustrations 1a, 1b, and 1d the upper chamber is located by a window frame or a crude 'scaffold', and access to it is simply by a ladder. In illustration 1c, the action revolves around a single chest. In all cases there is no indication of anything in the way of scenery or decoration, although in illustration 1c there is a hint of drapes beneath the scaffold and of painting on the upper stage framework.

The focus is always upon the actors, and their exaggerated actions within an open, uncomplicated, easily erected and transportable space.

The masks in all these paintings are positive and clearly defined as caricatures of stock characters. Thus displayed they would be instantly recognisable to their audience. Even in these paintings the physical attitudes of say the old men are similarly stated, suggesting that there was a common bodily language which identified age, anger, lust, scorn, etc.

The Fabula Atellana according to Phyllis Hartnoll

'... seems to have been designed to suit the taste of the crowds which gathered on markets days in country towns'. It had a 'recurring motif... of disguise and masquerade. It was a farce which displayed certain traditional

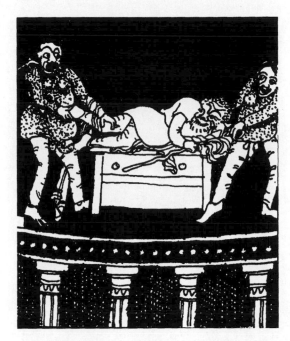

1(c). 4th-century Phylax vase painting, Staatliche Museen, Berlin

characters... such as the clowns Maccus and Bucco, the old fool Pappus, Manducus the ogre and Dossennus the hunchback, in ridiculous situations... such as might amuse a primitive and rustic audience, ever ready to laugh at guzzling and drunkenness, horseplay and obscene jest... These stock roles would require stock costumes and masks'.[3]

She also continues to describe the form and content of the farces as being short in length and containing few characters, and were probably 'impromptu' before they became fixed and included in literary form at the time of the 1st century B.C.

Because much of their farce contained many political references they were forced, through circumstance (namely execution) to return to a more mimetic form, despite their popularity with the masses.

During the next fourteen hundred years, despite the familiar moral intervention and control of 'entertainment' by the Church, the return of the Crusaders, the invasions of neighbouring adversaries, the theatre survived. In fact all these new experiences and the new-found knowledge of themes taken from the Old and New Testaments, furnished the Italians with more material to deride and use as subject matter for new farces, thus allowing for further derision of subject matter other than the familiar stories and characters in ancient mythology. Their humour became topical.

---

[3] Hartnoll, P. *Oxford Companion to the Theatre*, p. 304

1(d). 4th-century Phylax vase painting, British Museum, London

2. Commedia stage fit-up. Raised platform, sliding drapes, cloth and frame

So whilst there is much fact available which illustrates clearly the three forms I have described, there is little direct evidence to lay before the reader to say without doubt that the Satyr plays, the Phlyax dramas and the Fabula Atellana were all direct antecedents of the Commedia Dell'Arte, in the same way – for instance – that the Noh ancestry is so doubtlessly documented.

However, it is very clear that there is a base line of common ground which can be safely assumed to tie together these historical facts, and conclude that there is a recognisable genetic lineage, which congeals and blossoms, into a recognisable and increasingly better documented Commedia Renaissance. It is to this period that I shall extract my material to show the similarities between the Noh and the Commedia.

Most of my resource material is the same as that of theatre historians such as Pierre Louis Duchartre and Allardyce Nicoll. However there has been a refreshing move on the part of at least one Art historian, Ms M. A. Katritzky, who has devoted much time to look more closely at the visual material which has already been exhaustively referred to, and has added to this, information gleaned from her discovery of a number of sets of prints, engravings and paintings from which she has made some conclusive, comparative analysis.

Her main contention is that...

'only when the mass of surviving visual material, ranging from the ephemeral to works of the highest quality, has been published and put into art-historical context, will its potential as documentary evidence be available for interpretation by the theatre historian'.[4]

She is preoccupied with the accuracy of the content and the context of the visual material she has studied, and of correcting many inaccuracies in dating of original material. In one instance she describes how

'the ten works attributed to Lodewyk Toeput feature three distinct contexts in which the Italian comedians are found, namely, formal staged theatre performances, folk festivals and courtly celebrations, in both indoor and outdoor settings. A closer examination of these pictures provides an opportunity to consider these manifestations of the Commedia Dell'Arte in the context of visual depictions rather than by relying on the descriptions of contemporary spectators or even on indirect written evidence such as scenarios or second-hand reports'.[5]

She then continues with a most significant statement regarding the visual language of the Commedia actors by saying

---

[4] Katritzky, M. A. *Lodewyk Toeput; Some Pictures Related to the Commedia Dell'Arte* (Renaissance Studies, Volume I, Number 1, London 1988) p. 75
[5] Katritzky, M. A. p. 79

'certain aspects of the Commedia Dell'Arte, such as costume and gesture, are unquestionably capable of being more reliably recorded in pictures'.[6]

It has been my similar experience to conduct part of my own research into the style and skills of the Commedia actor, using the available pictorial evidence.

It has also been important for me to examine closely the earliest written versions of the scenarios as published in the *Teatro* of Flaminia Scala in 1611. There are many characters who repeatedly appear in most scenarios and I shall look briefly at the most familiar of these.

Stock Characters

These 'types, masks, caricatures' exist in the Commedia as representatives of their social standing not only in each narrative but in all communities in all times.

They sometimes work alone and sidle around groups like unnerving shadows causing havoc whenever situations dictate, or they operate as

3. Dottore

couples, partners, 'double acts' such as masters and mistresses with their servants or lovers and rich widows. Often these relationships interrelate.

The masters are often elderly, and are either merchants – usually 'eminent and Venetian' (*Pantalone*) – or doctors of law and 'learning' (*Dottore*). They are usually the butt of their servant's (and anyone else's) humour'.

They are sometimes the parents of the young man or woman in love, and they make their moral and parental contribution to the traditional love intrigue which permeates most of the Commedia narratives. They are also occasionally involved with their own chasing of women. They usually fail miserably, and this also adds considerably to the comedy.

Their servants or *zanni* are the mainstay of the Commedia tradition, and their enduring, historical development has remained a true testament to their perennial popularity. They are at the bottom of the social heap and usually are the characters who receive the greatest sympathy from the audience.

---

[6] Katritzky, M. A. p. 79

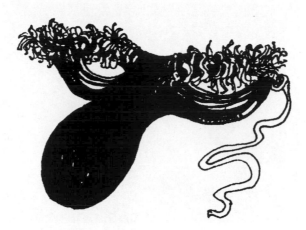

4. Dottore mask

They provide the humorous base which determines the breathless and often confused energy at the heart of the performance. The actors who play the zanni must have the consummate skills to shift the direction of the narrative and the comic devices, as and when they deem it necessary to do so, for the benefit of the continued attention and entertainment of their audience.

Their clowning contains ample displays of gymnastic fooling, obscene vulgarity, slick exchanges of verbal and physical repartee. Such is the style of their performance that their audience should be exhausted at its

5. Pantalone

6. Pantalone mask

conclusion because of the excesses of energised comic device. The most instantly recognisable and lasting characters to have emerged from the zannis are *Arlecchino* (Harlequin) and *Pulcinella* (Mr. Punch).

There are others, notably *Capitano* the braggart soldier who finds himself personified so delightfully in the familiar Falstaff, Captain Mainwaring or Sergeant Bilko characters. But the eternal cast of the Commedia remains with these important few.

7. Zanni

8. Arlecchino   9. Arlecchino mask

Some characters evolved with the actors who developed their 'type' and were so popular in their era the actor's family name became that of the character.

Here we may pause and consider the implications of the presence of

these 'stock' characters upon their audience – in terms of the actors playing them – and examine the reasons for their popularity.

Firstly the characters would be instantly recognisable even before they spoke. They would be identified by their mask, their accompanying costume (which would have its own identifiable colour-coding), their physical attitude and gait, props and accoutrements, as well as a linguistic association with a specific geographical and cultural location.

Pantalone, a middle-aged – but still energetic Venetian – may support a brown mask, red tights and jacket, a black cloak, and tucked in his belt would be a sword and a handkerchief. *Brighella* from Bergamo but turned Neapolitan, could be decked

10. Pulcinella

11. Pulcinella mask

from head to toe in green, supporting a sword which he would often use to great effect; he was a man with 'a special weakness for quarrels'.

Arlecchino, one of the zanni, could have a black mask, a patchwork jacket and tights: sometimes he would support an animated beard, and may carry a slapstick... and so on.

They would be greeted as old friends to laugh with and embrace, or familiar enemies to be ridiculed and harangued.

12. Capitano

13. Capitano mask

The actor would probably only play one character all his acting life, occasionally assuming another only to accommodate illness or injury. This singular devotion to one character meant that he could concentrate entirely upon those elements of speech and action which proved to be the most effective in performance, discovered through the familiar experience of testing by trial and error with different audiences.

It is safe to assume then, that the characters, similar to those of the Noh, were already known and established. How the actor embellished and

14. Traditional Commedia properties

added skills which produced freshness and novelty to these basic characteristics, determined their popularity or otherwise as professionals. This of course is still true today. Witness the fondness with which once familiar comedians and their characters are gorged and spat out in favour of fresh fodder by the discerning public.

These stock characters moved through the familiar territory of plotting and intrigue, changing and adapting to each other and the situation accordingly. The size of the company of characters was usually between ten and twelve, but whereas Shakespeare's company was compatible in size and skills with the Commedia troupe, they would expect to do a lot of 'doubling' given the number of characters in Shakespeare's plays. The Commedia actor was likely to only play one character.

Thus, the number of characters in a Commedia performance was determined by the number of actors in the company, and provides another reason why the characters became so familiarly 'stock'.

15. Isabella and the more traditional 'loup'

Whilst the female characters such as Isabella sometimes wore *loups* but did not wear masks, I have usually designed a character mask for these roles in order that the physicality of the acting style determined by the mask remains consistent throughout the cast.

The male lovers such as *Flavio* were similarly unmasked.

The Scenarios

The comic language of Commedia is not written and fixed in the familiar, scripted sense. It is carried in the heads of the actors and handed down from generation to generation, much in the same way that jokes or anecdotes are passed on (and altered and embellished to match contemporary events) from person to person.

What was written down for the benefit of the actors during the performance, was a list – similar to the Elizabethan 'platt' – of the running order of scenes; their position in the narrative, the briefest of descriptions of their content – what each character does – the number of characters included in each scene, and the entrances and exits which effect the transition of each scene. There is not one word of dialogue, although there is an indication of the content of an exchange between characters. These 'lists' are called *scenarios*.

Each scenario is subdivided, usually into three, similarly sized acts, which may include as many as ten or twelve short scenes. Each scene consists of an exchange between two or, very occasionally, three characters, as well as a musing monologue or exposition.

Given all the familiar master/mistress and servant, love and intrigue pairings, it is possible to permutate a seemingly endless combination of different 'double-acts' and trios. Thus a 'script' could be collated which included a continuous stream of fresh interaction. The possibilities appear endless.

If we read through the extant scenarios of Flaminia Scala which were printed in 1611, it is a simple matter to establish that the main theme which permeates each scenario is one which contains a love intrigue. The play will usually end with a happy resolution of this intrigue for the young lovers, but the ageing decrepits their lusts and fantasies – always at the centre of the cruel teasing by the zannis – usually go unrequited.

However it is not so easy to sort out the many different layers of plot and plotting which weave their unchartered way through most of the scenarios. Quite often, just as the mind of the audience screams for a respite from the complex and seemingly arbitrary interlacing of the many 'sprung hares', one of the zannis would play a ridiculous scene allowing the audience just enough space to clear their minds and return refreshed and ready for the plot to continue.

And yet it is difficult to imagine that the Commedia would survive for two centuries, if the stock characters were merely to repeat the same stock situations and the same simple framework of character. There are as many different nuances of character and situation as there are scenarios. What the Commedia enabled the actor to do was to extend his knowledge and development of character over a lifetime of playing that single character, rather than having to discover and present a single character within the time scale of the singular production of a scripted, two and a half hour play.

There will be fights, beatings, lies, cheating, mocking, mimicry, knock-about and slapstick, topical references to particularise those locally (who may be identified by the action) music, magic, tumbling (of a standard which we would associate with circus) and enough coarse vulgarity to make our present day blue jokes seem naïve.

At its heart, the action would be painful to the victim. For me, Commedia exemplifies the comedy of derision.

It is the kind of comedy which has filtered through generations of double-acts and which can be readily identified in our own Music-hall tradition. Each interaction is devised, learned, honed to perfection regarding timing and delivery, tried and tested in as wide a variety of arena as possible, and then fixed and used in that final form, within a programme of pre-planned lists of similarly tried and tested comic devices or narratives. All this is carried in the head, and includes the cues which signal the delivery of each device or routine. The 'gag' rests in the subconscious and is triggered by the cues.

In Commedia language, the version of the 'gag' is either a *'lazzo'* or a lengthier and more complex version called a *'burle'*. The lazzo, at its simplest, is a funny moment, which may be repeated as and when it is necessary. It may be a 'funny walk' or a complex and classical version of the 'Eating of the Fly' lazzo of Arlecchino. It might be a quick and amusing bout of tumbling or crazy gymnastics, juggling or sword-play. But its main feature is that it can be used at any time the actor thinks the action needs enlivening, or changing quickly to re-engage the focus of the audience.

It is not therefore just a popular and assumed part of a particular character's personal, theatrical characteristic. It forms a crucial part of the comic's 'up the sleeve' armoury.

The burle (from which is derived the familiar form 'Burlesque') is a more complex and more deeply plot-affecting device, like a practical joke, which can change the whole course of events in the narrative; such as the metamorphosis (by the drinking of a magic potion encouraged by Arlecchino) of say Pulcinella, into a dog, and all the derisive comic action that ensues, until the effect of the potion has worn off and comic revenge is plotted and executed.

The main aspect of these lazzis and burles is that they would be most thoroughly prepared and rehearsed and honed, so that in performance they could almost certainly guarantee a favourable response from the

16. Lazzo sequence 1

17. Lazzo sequence 2

audience. Such a 'stockpile' would take years to learn and assemble, and would most certainly be jealously guarded from plagiarist rivals.

Which brings me logically to the single most familiar aspect of the Commedia which seems to have been adopted by teachers of drama and acting, and that is the art of *improvisation*. It is this singular term that I want to briefly address my attention so that I may allay the many assumptions and misconceptions concerning the improvisation technique. The unique hallmark of the technique of the Commedia actor in performance is his reliance upon his skill with the mask and his ability at improvisation.

Improvisation

'The influence of the Commedia Dell'Arte on the theatre of Europe is incalculable'.[7]

So it could also be said of 'Improvisation' when referring to the methodology employed in the teaching of Drama in educational institutions in the West. In many of the more familiar publications on Drama there is an inevitable chapter on Improvisation. *Improvisation*,[8] the book by Hodgson and Richards, is a pocket bible for teachers of curriculum drama. In Actor-Training centres like The Bristol Old Vic Theatre School, and the Central School of Speech and Drama, 'Improvisation' technique forms an important part of the training syllabus.

---

[7] Hartnoll, P. *A Concise History of the Theatre* p. 68
[8] Hodgson, J. and Richards, E. *Improvisation: Discovery and Creativity in Drama* (Methuen, 1966)

It can be assumed therefore, that in the West, generations of actors, directors and audiences know and understand the meaning and use of the term 'Improvisation'. It is associated with a release of ideas, presented in the form of a spontaneous outpouring of dialogue and action, which has evolved within the boundaries of 'play' – or more precisely – character narratives and 'role-play'.

A situation or stimulus is introduced and its consequence is explored or 'played' out until such time as the impetus of the original stimulus tires, and a new stimulus evolves or is set – and so on. The stimulus is shared and explored by those taking part, which may or may not include an audience. Nothing is set down in the form of dialogue and direction in the familiar sense of a script, although the germ of a plan, a direction, may be introduced; its 'novelty' and energy being generated by the notion of exploration and adventure.

It is this freedom from working with a rigid form of 'text' which participants in improvisation sessions find both liberating and daunting. It is usually associated with the spontaneous exploration of dialogue for those who find scriptwriting too rigidly contrived and practically restricting.

However, there is no sense in which 'Improvised' theatre is a familiar part of the professional theatrical *performance* in the West. By that, I mean that it is rare to see a play in which all the action and dialogue by the actors is improvised.

Some of what I have described, would be familiar to the Commedia actor. But I suspect that his interpretation of 'freedom' when applied to his version of improvisation would have a different emphasis. This difference is vital if we are to understand the way in which the Commedia actor prepares for, and accomplishes his performance.

We in Britain, associate Improvisation with work unfinished and unpolished; work in progress: a process of exploration which sometimes leads to the discovery of a way of clarifying an erstwhile dramatic complexity or problem. Sometimes, the process of improvisation leads a playwright, director, or actor (permutate any combination of these) to the final language of a play, which in turn is then presented to its audience and repeated in the form of its fixed and finished script; improvisation as a means, rather than an end.

Companies like Joint Stock, The early Hull Truck, and even the Royal Shakespeare Company (Nicholas Nickleby) immediately come to mind, who have achieved high public acclaim for distinctively fresh work which has been devised using improvisation techniques. Apart from the belief that this process is profitable to the actor/writer/director as an important process of discovery, there is little skill – in the finished performance sense – that is associated with it; usually the reverse.

To subject a company of actors, carrying their improvised role – playing directly to their audience, would be considered far too risky and extremely self-indulgent.

So what was different about the actor and audiences of the Renaissance which made their 'celebration' of theatre seem so energised, accessible and highly skilled?

The actors of the Commedia Dell'Arte 'improvised' in the sense that they were able to follow and interpret even the most hastily conceived scenario. Hours of performance were developed in the acting space, in front of an audience, from two or three pages of scenario. The 'Improvisation' technique of the Commedia actor, to fulfil this seemingly impossible task with any degree of success, needed to employ considerable skill if the attention of the audience was to be sustained.

Before I make a conjectural assessment of the Commedia Improvisation technique in detail, it may be worth while to look aside for a moment and examine the work of Peter Brook, who has always used improvisation as a tool of reference in the exploration of his work with actors. It is interesting to recall his attitude to English actors in the early seventies when he was recording his views on his production of US with the Royal Shakespeare Company. Even in 1970, improvisation was a familiar rehearsal technique.

> 'Ten years ago, to get a group of English actors to improvise on any theme would have been extremely difficult; the most prominent thing you'd come up against would be the English actor's unwillingness to throw himself into something unchartered... Today we find that to ask a group of actors who have worked together to do scenes of torture, brutality, violence and madness is frighteningly easy and frighteningly pleasurable for all of us. The thing takes off and moves and develops with quite alarming ease'.[9]

A few years later, once he was settled with his company of actors at the Bouffes Du Nord, and sponsored by the International Centre of Theatre research in Paris, Peter Brook embarked upon a three month epic journey through Africa with a company of actors, auxiliaries and crew. In his account of this journey – revealed in an interview with Michael Gibson – the most often used word when describing the experimental process was 'Improvisation'. Time after time, in community after community, the carpet was unrolled, the acting area defined, and the 'improvisation' begun. This small account of an African journey reveals much first hand experience about the nature of performance, performer and audience.

On 'improvisation' Brook is absolutely clear.

---

[9] Brook, P. *The Shifting Point* (Methuen, 1988) p. 62

'We have learned that improvisation is an exceptionally difficult and precise technique and very different from the generalised idea of a spontaneous 'happening'. Improvisation requires great skill on the part of the actors in all aspects of theatre. It requires specific training and also great generosity and a great capacity for humour. Genuine improvisation, leading up to a real encounter with the audience, only occurs when the spectators feel that they are loved and respected by the actors. We have learned that for this reason improvised theatre must go to where people live'.[10]

The discoveries made by these intrepid travellers and recorded by Brook, for me makes a direct and emotional link with the Commedia companies of the Renaissance.

The difference between Brook's company, engaged on this particular experiment, and that of the Commedia troupes, is that Brook's actors and their audience were unknown to each other: the Commedia troupes on the other hand, would not only present well loved characters in a familiar narrative, but there is a likelihood that their audiences would be located on a well-trodden seasonal circuit. That doesn't mean that Brook faced his 'tour' anticipating a negative response. Nor did he receive one.

'We have also learned that groups of people living in a form of isolation, like immigrants in France, are astonished and touched when actors come to them quite simply and play in their familiar places. The greatest tact and sensitivity are needed to avoid giving the impression that their intimacy is invaded. If there is no sense of an act of charity, only the feeling that one group of human beings wants to make contact with another, then theatre becomes life in a more concentrated form. Without theatre, a lot of strangers meeting one another would not get very far in a short time. But the additional energies released by singing, dancing and playing out conflicts, and by excitement and laughter, are so great that in a single hour amazing things can happen... This effect is particularly intense if the group of actors include people with different backgrounds. With an international company, a deep understanding can be touched between people who seem to have nothing in common'.[11]

One of the most interesting discoveries of this experiment is that the response to the 'improvisations' was at its best when there was a preparation of material which may or may not be used.

'The more we took the total risk, and went into villages prepared for everything but having no idea at all of what we were going to do, the freer, in fact, we got from any sort of structure or idea, the better the result always was... the more that risk was taken, the better the results. Something always

---

[10] Brook, P. p. 112
[11] Brook, P. pp. 113–114

created itself, that really was influenced, second by second, by the presence of the people, the time of day, the light – all of those reflected themselves in the best performances. And themes that we'd worked on in the past would recur in a different place, a different order and a different manner... And when, because something had worked, we tried to repeat it (often just through laziness, tiredness, or through not thinking), the result was less good'.[12]

I have quoted Peter Brook because his thoughts and reflections about his improvised experiments have been extensively recorded in print. What he has written has the smell of Commedia about it. What Brook describes in detail, is the setting up of a performance space, in a community, by a travelling band of highly trained, professional performers.

'A group of people, from different parts of the world [had] set out to discover if a human contact could be made through a particular form called theatre'.[13]

Once the pair of shoes were placed in the centre of the circle 'something needed to happen. Everybody was looking at a spot where, someone having performed one action, a further action was expected'.[14]

In summarising the skills of the Commedia actor we must assume that at the heart of his technique is the singular asset of 'Improvisation'.

At the conclusion to his chapter on 'Improvisation' Allardyce Nicoll cites much authenticated evidence from contemporary comment, 'that the better Commedia actors...

... have so great skill in making use of such conceits that what has been carefully memorised seems to be wholly the result of their improvisation... (which) offers scope for variety in the action; you can go again and again to see the same play and each time it will be different... the actors come and go, speak and move as though they were at home... a naturalness and truth which the very finest playwrights rarely attain'.[15]

What are these skills?

Firstly, the scenarios described by Flaminia Scala suggest that usually the stage was occupied by only one or two actors at one time, and that when a third arrived, it was only to effect a change of action and scene – and was subject to the utmost brevity.

'Those characteristics of the scenario which enable it to control and direct the dramatic action so as to limit the dangers of complexity which might arise should the actors be given freer rein to explore the exponential

---

[12] Brook, P. pp. 117–118
[13] Brook, P. p. 120
[14] Brook, P. p. 118
[15] Nicoll, A. *The World of Harlequin* (Cambridge University Press, 1963) p. 39

possibilities of interaction... these characteristics... rather than inhibiting improvisation, seemed to facilitate it'.[16]

We need to be reminded that a Commedia actor would usually perform only one character in his or her acting career. So he would carry in his armoury a 'store... of philosophical sayings, poetic conceits, pleas of love, reproofs, despairs, frenzies – which [to] have on hand for various occasions'[17] and which would be totally and recognisably associated with that singular character.

He could refine, and test his material as he toured from place to place adding and subtracting local reference according to where and to whom he performed. Once he was convinced that his character, his 'act', contained enough reference points of security to which he could always rely, he could launch into any improvisation with a similarly prepared actor, with a heightened sense of 'disciplined' freedom.

He would so 'become' the character he was playing, that he would be able to plot his route confidently through a narrative, adapting his material according to the scenario, and according to the response of the audience.

Within the necessary boundaries of the scenario, and his skill, he was at liberty to 'improvise' in open collaboration with his fellow actors in a singular attempt to embrace his audience. He exercised his wit and his character with those who had gathered to shake his hand and share his adventure.

What I have described, using a conjectural reconstruction based on the facts of extant illustrations, letters and scenarios, needed – in my view – a practical exploration which may confirm or otherwise the views that I have so far expressed.

With a small company of four student actors I embarked upon a four week rehearsal and performance period of a newly written masked commedia called *Please Be Gentle*. My journal kept during this rehearsal period is a completely subjective account, as I recognise that at best, it remains in academic terms, a somewhat fragile experiment. However, as I progressed, evaluating carefully the significance of the conjectural process, I became confident in the knowledge that I was making a familiar journey with the mask.

The main difference between this play and the performance of a traditional scenario is that the dialogue and the lazzi are written down in textual form. My reason for this was that at the heart of my experiment was a need explore the potential of the physical resources demanded of this comic style, rather than devote most of the rehearsal period devising

---

[16] Lorch, J. Italian Institute Pamphlet. 'Pirandello, Commedia Dell'Arte and Improvisation' (London, 1988)
[17] Nicoll, A. *The World of Harlequin* p. 39

a method of creating the spoken comic language in an improvised way during the performance. This I felt was an unrealistic task.

I was confident, that I could create a linguistic style appropriate to the stock characters, which would be simple to learn, and would help to support the physical language required by the mask. A compromise, but not one which I felt would interfere too much with the spirit of the Commedia.

In any case, I was especially inquisitive about the effect of the mask in a play written in a more traditional western style. I consoled my doubts by writing into the script all the commedia elements I could think of both traditionally and contemporarily. I wanted to test not only the structure of the comic elements but also its perennial social reference.

So, the script included numerous newly-devised lazzi, a tangle of love intrigue, a clearly defined class structure, an assortment of comic style which matched slapstick with cynical wit, a continuous list of double-acts, separated into twenty-six short scenes – about the average number of scenes which fill a Scala scenario – and unnerving moments of violent anarchy to add spice to the breathless exchanges of dialogue.

To accommodate the traditional western 'Interval' the play was divided into two parts. On reflection this turned out to be a fortuitous move, for the actors found that they could just about survive for the length of each half, given the exacting style demanded by the mask in performance. Fifteen scenes of approximately three minutes' duration was as much as they could sustain.

I included a strong Punch and Judy element to obviate a derivative link with the traditional commedia, and this also influenced the colourful booth-like quality of the design.

Most important of all I included in the directions all the detailed physical choreography implicit in the exchanges and the narrative, to determine unequivocally the profound influence of the mask.

PLEASE BE GENTLE: AN INTRODUCTION

I was fortunate that the cast included three professional performers and one very talented amateur. A member of the Syrian National Theatre, Fayez Kazak, played Punch, Melanie Jones played Judy, an Indian storyteller Vayu Naidu played Herself, and Chris Banfield played Himself. All were members of The Workshop Theatre of the University of Leeds, and were post-graduate students.

The title of the piece already has ironic connotations in western terms, of a joking yet violent, sexist, associations with the loss of virginity. Given that the main zanni character is *Punch* and the subrette is *Judy* (our main existing derivation from the Commedia) the 'gentle' irony assumes larger proportions.

The two other characters from the Ruling class, are the husband and wife duo, *Himself* and *Herself*. Thus, in character terms, the script contains a traditional Commedia master/servant reference, and, in consequence, a small but significant potential for permutating a variety of comic 'double-acts'.

The *plot* is simple. Punch, bored, embarks upon a catastrophic journey of gleeful destruction, which finally ends in his 'marriage' to Judy. En route, a garden, a household and its occupants are vandalised, a baby is traditionally battered within an inch of its life, and the vindictiveness within allegedly loving relationships is openly and savagely 'ripped to bits'. An invitation it would seem, to explore the 'comedy of derision'.

None of the actors had worked in this way with mask before. I decided that each actor would be closely involved with the making of his or her own mask.

Using the 'gypsona' method, described in Appendix (ii) of Volume 1, casts were made of the upper half of the actor's face, and the elements of the characters built up in relief in gumstrip two or three weeks before the rehearsal process began. There was also the opportunity (and the expectancy) that during rehearsals, the detail of the personality characteristics on the masks, would alter subtly according to the many sides of each character discovered by the actors during the rehearsal process. By working in this way the actors had a constant reference to the character of their mask.

Each character eventually became more or less fixed in the design of their mask during rehearsals. The clearer and simpler the design of the mask, the better the actor was able to embrace the character. The mask was the character. Within its design lay a list of characteristics to which the actor could always refer. It was his constant resource.

In this small experimental group, during the whole rehearsal process, it became the norm for actors struggling with the detail of character and the behaviour of that character to return to the mask for ideas.

That didn't mean that the design of the mask was so fixed that the character could only become animated in a small range of physical attitudes and gestures. The mask for Punch for instance was so simple in design that it looked to have a very limited range of expression. In fact it was this very simplicity which made its psychological potential so versatile in the hands of an experienced actor like Fayez.

I am reminded of the Ko-omote (Young Woman) mask of the Noh. Its features are so smooth and soft and simply defined. It is this open simplicity which belies its enormous range of expression. In general, the less fixed the expression of the mask the more enigmatic and versatile its potential.

Within its design also is included the repeat patterns of angularity – eyebrow, cheek, hairline, etc. – which identifies the 'body design' of the physical attitudes adopted by the actor wearing the mask.

In the early rehearsals, much time was spent searching for this new attitude, which, when developed, would form the basis of the travelling motion and rhythms of the character. The mask instantly demands that the wearer finds a new body rhythm. I cannot stress too strongly that in all the many experiments of this kind which I have conducted, this is always the case.

It is almost the opposite when asking an unmasked actor to think positively about the physical attitude and rhythms of a character. In this production, the actors learned to walk, stand, sit, stride, lean, lie, and exchange dialogue, displaying a physical rhythm totally new to them as actors; they discovered how to animate their mask by energising the complementary language of their bodies.

Having established the physical rhythms of the character and a framework of reference anchored in the mask, the next stage was to become liberated within this framework, to use it and adjust it according to the other framework of the narrative.

Each actor built up a mental scenario of physical contacts and keys which were sparked off by encounters with other characters. Like a musical score, the tone, texture, colour and rhythm of each duo, was discovered and explored, and finally established in a working framework for performance.

Each mask had its accompanying prop and costume. *Punch* wielded his trusty slapstick and made many ludicrous shapes with his floppy tall hat and the long sleeves which dangled from his shirt. *Judy* wore her turban and deeply pocketed apron; both were constantly wrung and twisted in anger and frustration. *Himself* had his floppy-eared deerstalker cap and zipped, shallow-pocketed body-warmer from which his head and his hands were rarely removed, giving him the look of a mouldy Beagle, whilst *Herself* wore a long, swishing gown which seemed to crackle and hiss with each movement of her serpent-like body.

The acting space resembled – coincidently – in scale and shape, a Noh space. Because of the architecture of the church which contained the space designated for performance, the audience sat on two adjoining sides of the twenty-foot acting square as they do for a performance of Noh. This meant that for each 'facet' of audience the actors had to give equal consideration to the profile presentation of their mask. This simple, but obvious fact, helped to determine a three-dimensional awareness on the part of the performer.

A candy-striped booth occupied the upstage corner, reminding us of the Punch and Judy, cloth-and-frame booth of the beaches. Apart from this, the set was simple and relatively empty, having a number of small, easily moveable child-block cuboids which could be added, subtracted to, and built within the space as required by the actors.

They suggested rather than represented necessary 'furniture'. The emptiness of the space allowed for the choreographed movement, in the same uncluttered way that is the norm for dance. When not in use, they were arranged around the periphery of the square.

When the actors were not included in a short scene they sat on these cuboids, turned away from their audience closing down their mask. Their proximity to the acting space enabled instant, and explosive access. It became very clear to the audience that the acting space was a special space which seemed to magically activate those who entered into and occupied it.

Again, it was ironic that I discovered the quality of this space before my African-influenced masked experiment, and before I touched the hallowed boards of a Noh stage.

At this point I wish to offer an important discovery which I made as I have revived and re-activated recollections from my rehearsal notes.

There is something about the animation of a mask which is distinctive and special, and I am convinced that it has a lot to do with a recognisable re-incarnation of a character of a previous life. It is only now, in retrospect, having studied the Noh, that I see all masks as ghosts. The space in which they inhabit has a different ethereal quality. I can't describe it, but I know it's there and I instantly recognise it. If the performance of the mask is convincing then I think the audience feels it too. There is a sense then in which all characters in any drama, with or without the physical wearing of masks are ghosts re-incarnated.

However, the Commedia ghost is a comic ghost. It is to this side of his ghostliness that I shall remain for a moment. I shall describe some of the comic challenge presented to the actors in *Please be Gentle* and, in particular, the working of two of the lazzi.

The first concerns the second scene of the play and introduces the audience to *Judy*.

> *JUDY enters and dives into a dozen jobs at once and only just managing to satisfy the needs of all of them: a bit like a scuttling balancing act with spinning plates.*
>
> *She mixes pastry, checks the vegetables cooking on the stove, mops the floor, washes the pots etc., the central focus of all of this mayhem is the baby, who is squawling; the squawls come from one of the chorus.**

During the sequence the baby is blamed for every catastrophe that almost occurs, and is silenced by beating. Judy rushes around attending to all the elements in turn, muttering to herself, bewailing her lot. The kitchen 'elements' are arranged on the periphery of the square, like a drum kit with cymbals, and the consequential flurry of manic movement resembles that of the late Keith Moon of 'The Who'.

In addition to all of this is the placing of the dialogue which is written in such a way that the tempo of the scene can be clearly registered; the scuttling feet and the repetition of the actions contrive to beat out the rhythm of the scene. All of this is designed to resemble a lazzo.

The lazzo is the 'always-got-too-much-to-do' side of Judy's personality. Once established, it can be applied to many different situations and reconstituted accordingly. Setting the table and attending to the final touches of the dinner being another example of its application. It is a lazzo which can be pulled out of the repertoire of other lazzi whenever it is needed.

It was during the working of these lazzi that the actors learned the art of 'fixing' and not blurring the mask.

Despite the speed with which many of the lazzi are played, the general effect of the scene is determined by the clarity of the mask. The angles of the head and the body, the 'placing' of limbs according to the correct setting of the mask is of vital importance. Time and time again the actors lost the meaning of the mask mainly through lack of concentration and focus.

What they eventually appreciated most of all, was to recognise behind their mask, the need for a clearly defined set of key signals, which they and their mask were sending to their audience. Learning the precise placing of the body to display accurately these signals, and to be able to repeat them time and time again, was the singularly most arduous part of the rehearsal process.

One of the most delightful discoveries which the actors made, was, that after a while, they could apply their newly discovered knowledge of their masks to any new encounter with another mask.

---

*See *Please Be Gentle*, p. 37

To see the rhythms and movement of each character stimulated by the cut and thrust of a fast exchange of comic dialogue, was to catch hints of some of the more beautiful dancing rituals of animal courtship. The language and the masks and the bodies were in complete harmony – just for a few seconds at a time. What was even more gratifying was that the audience caught these glimpses also – and laughed.

PLEASE BE GENTLE

A masked Commedia

CHARACTERS

PUNCH	An unemployed idiot
HIMSELF	A landowner having a large house and garden
HERSELF	His wife
JUDY	Her Cook, Nanny and general do-for

THE SET

Large playing blocks and planks.
The characters change the set scene by scene, creating the 'Playing Environments' intimated in the directions.
The permanent feature is a larger-than-life Punch and Judy booth, which offers an upper level.
The characters emerge at the beginning, and stand or sit in the shadows, heads inclined away from the square, so that they are out of mask. They remain as a physical, choral presence in the shadows and only assist vocally when not included in a scene. Once the characters move, they animate their mask. All properties are established and located by suggestive dialogue, and unless indicated otherwise, are mimed.

18. *Please Be Gentle* set

(a) Herself

(b) Judy

(c) Himself

(d) Punch

19. Mask designs for *Please Be Gentle*

SCENE ONE – A Grey Room with a Fireless Hearth

Cheerless. Slumped astride a chair back-to-front, head resting on overlapped hands and arms spanning the backrest, is PUNCH. Attached to, and dangling from a wrist like the tail of an angry cat, is a long, well-used slapstick – all he has to play with. He is bored.

PUNCH: (*Growling, quietly*) Dooty dooty doo. Dooty dooty doo. What to do? Whata whata whata whatado?

(*Pause*)

Dooty dooty doo. (*Still quiet threatening. Suddenly daft. Mock tears.*) Sad. *Very* sad. Nobody. Nobody in the whole entire world. Every day, every night, every week, every month, every year, all day long all by myself no one to talk to no one to sing to no one to dance to no one to eat to no one to set fire with... no one to light the fire *in*. Worst of, worst of all no one to shout at. If I had someone to shout at... if I had someone to *shout* at I could... (*Stands up slowly, with menace, gripping the slapstick in both hands*). If they, *if* they like it, and especially if they didn' I could... (*Aims a savage cracking blow at the back of the chair. Is about to aim another, but changes his mind in mid-aim and slowly sinks to his former position, trembling, depressed, bored as before*). Dooty dotty doo...

He stands slightly, the chair lifts with him as he shuffles with it suspended between his straddled legs, to one of the corners and settles. His bent back becomes the table on which JUDY mixes the pastry

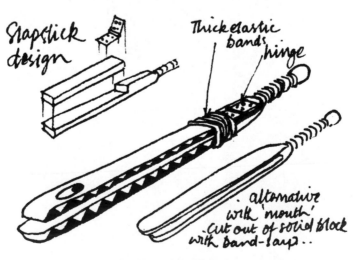

20. Slapstick design

SCENE TWO – The Kitchen of the Great House of HIMSELF and HERSELF

JUDY enters and dives into a dozen jobs at once and only just managing to satisfy the needs of all of them: a bit like a scuttling balancing act with spinning plates.

She mixes pastry, checks the vegetables cooking on the stove, mops the floor, washes the pots etc., the central focus of all of this mayhem is the baby, who is squawling; the squawls come from one of the chorus.

JUDY: (*To self*) Dear oh dear oh dear. Punch Punch Punch. Little bit of this, little bit of that. In with the water. Mix... Punch Punch Punch. Feed the baby.

Grabs a bottle, dashes to the cot and thrusts the bottle into the baby's squawling mouth

Ugh!

Holds her nose as she rushes to the linen basket and begins tossing unironed washing everywhere

Change his nappy.

21. Judy

Finds one, rushes back to the baby and rips off the soiled nappy

Yucky mucky shitbag!

Stuffs the clean nappy in the baby's mouth silencing it for a second or two before it begins squawling again

Sleep. That's what's wrong with you. Tired. Sleep! (*Belts baby*) There's a good baby. Who's a good baby then? (*Baby resumes squawling*) You're not! (*Belts baby*) Good baby! (*Baby squawls*) Please yourself! (*Belts baby. Baby squawls*) Off to sleep! (*Belts baby. Baby squawls*) Sleep sleep sleep! (*Baby silent*) There. Good baby. Tired weren't you? (*Beats it once more for good measure*) Yes. Now then... Oh dear! (*Notices that the water is running over the edge of the sink*) Oh dear. Out with the plug. (*Plunges hand into the boiling water*) Owwwwww! Naughty water naughty water! (*Belts water*) Hot hot hot! Naughty water! (*Water subsides*) That's better. Nice water. (*Strokes water*) Nice water nice water. Now then. (*Looks around for the next task and scuttles to the stove*) Look at the dinner. (*Pans boiling over furiously*) Oh... dinny dinny dinny (*Tastes it*) Too much salt, not enough pepper. (*Turns the heat down*) Better! Now then... (*Tastes again*) Pep it up a bit. (*Shakes pepper-pot extravagantly*) There we are. Little bit of pepper, oh yessy yessy yessy. (*More pepper*) Little bit of pepper pep it up a bit! (*Tastes it and coughs violently*) That's better. (*Looks for next task*) Ohh... (*Mess on the floor*) Look at the mess, look at it! (*Looks toward the cot*) Your fault! (*Rushes to the cot*) Your fault. (*Belts the baby. Baby squawls*) Now look what you've done! (*Looks at the floor and then for a mop*) Got to mop it up mop it up mop it up (*Does do with same extravagance*) That's better. Now then (*Pauses a moment*) Where was I? Ohhhhh yes...

Belts baby en route to the table where she continues with the pastry

Dear oh dear oh dear. Punch Punch Punch, little bit of this, little bit of that (*Looks at everything*) What am I going to do? (*And finally at the squawling baby*) What *am* I going to do?

She scuttles to the booth and climbs into it belting the baby in passing.

SCENE THREE

PUNCH as before, astride his chair, with his slapstick oscillating

PUNCH: What to do? What a do? Whatawhatawhata... think. That's it... think!

Pauses for a moment before cracking the slapstick as though he has hit himself on his head. The movement is very quick. Startling. Only the slapstick seems to move

Think! (*Another hit*) Think! (*Another hit*) Come on little nut do yer stuff, sort it out wakey wakey.
(*Simultaneously hitting his head. Rapid fire*) Think think think! (*Pause. Pained look evolves*) Aaaaaagh!

Pained look becomes grotesque and changes into an even more grotesque smile

Wait a minute. (*Sudden inspiration*) I know (*Cracks slapstick like a whip*) I've got it! (*Another crack. He screws up his body into a sequence of grotesque contortions before acting out an extraordinary violent attack on an imaginary victim with his slapstick. He slowly returns to his original posture and problem*)

Can't do that.

Ohhhh... what to do

Goes back to the chair and cocks one leg over the seat as though to sit and freezes, looking like a dog about to piss. This inspires him

I got it.

Runs around. Searching. Stops. Frozen.

No I'aven't.

Big sigh. Slow dissolve to the original posture

Oh dear. Deary deary me. (*Sudden burst of laughter. Stops laughing*) Nothing to laugh at. (*Laughs again, stops*) Nothing to laugh at! (*Laughs again*) Stop it stop it

Lifts slapstick as though to inflict real pain on himself. Suddenly, inspiration. Cracks slapstick like a whip.

I know! (*Hideous excitement*) Yyyeees! Got it! I have a good woo. Oh yyyyes. That's what I need. A little bit of woo. Go an' woo Judy. She my girl. Ohhhh yes! (*Cracks slapstick*) All by herself in that big house, all alone, all day, all night. Dooty dooty doo, I go for a woo (*To self*) Hey, that rhyme... dooty dooty doo...

Stands contemplating beneath the sill of the booth

SCENE FOUR–(*Continuing*)

JUDY appears above the sill slowly, like a glove puppet. Head down. Big glum.

JUDY: Fed up! Really fed up! All day, all night, beck and call, always at it, on me own, do this, do that, fed up! Now... *now*, when I've got a bit of time to myself, what am I doing? Nothing nothing *No... thing*! Fed up, fed up, fed up!

Sudden inspiration

I know! (*Even bigger inspiration*)... know what I'll do. Make myself look beeoootiful. That's what I'll do. Beeoootiful Judy.

Mimes a mirror, and a jewellery box and its contents which she places on the sill. She then opens the lid of the box with much glee

Ooooo. what 'ave we got 'ere? (*Powder puff*) Got to 'ave some of that (*applies it liberally*) oo yesee yesee. (*Finds a lipstick*) And little bit of that (*Applies it with abandon*)... and (*Eye-liner*) plenty of that (*Exaggerated lines*) and... (*Peers in box*) where is it? (*Peers closer*) where is it? where've you gone?

Begins tossing everything out of the box in all directions

Where are you?!

Scream of glee as she notices her mop cap which has been hanging up on the corner of the booth all the time

There you are you little rascal! (*Snatches it*) Beeoootiful!

Tries it on. Peers into the mirror breathing on it

Shit!

Removes her cap and cleans the mirror, turns away, puts her hat on and returns to face the mirror with her hands covering her eyes, playing with the moment of revelation

Now then *now then*! 'S'ave a look!

(*Removes hands from eyes*) Oooooo. Ooooo. (*Excess of pleasure*) Ooooooah, oooooahsay. Pretty Judy. Oh yes. Better now. Much better. Ooooooah-say...

Scuttles to the back of the booth out of sight

SCENE FIVE

PUNCH breaks out of his contemplation. Beside himself with anticipation.

PUNCH: Ooooo this is going to be good. See what you make of this Judy Judy Judy.

Pause while he sets himself

Now then... oooooooohhhh (*Sudden cowardice*) Can't do it. Oooooooohhhh deary deary me. (*Quietly. Head dropping*) Dooty dooty doo. (*Sudden inspiration*) I know. I'll have a practice. A practice woo. Now then.

Adopts a grotesque 'thinking' posture

Let's see. Say something... some... thing... nice! (*Vomits*) Can't. Can't do that. Upset me. (*Thinks*) But I got to do it if I want to woo. So... how about...

Develops a wooing posture. Should see it passing through his body until it establishes itself. Very grotesque. Clears his throat

Jooooooooooooody. Oh Jooooooooooody. I think you're Beeeoooooooooooti-ful (*Vomits*) That's no good. Kill me will that. (*Thinks*) Got it.

(*Prepares. As before... and vomits*) Oh dear, Whata do whata do?

Thinks. Sudden inspiration. Wooing posture as before

Right (*Slapstick*) Tell her about her pretty bits, that's what I'll do. Right. (*Wooing posture*) Oh Joooooooody. Judy Judy Joooooooody. I think your hair, your HAIR is glistens like a pan script. Your... eyes look out of your head like two lumps of coke, (*Getting carried away now*) Your nose wrinkles like a rabbit sniffing horse-shit, and your lips, your *lips* open and shut like a constipated trout! (*Relaxes*) That should do it. Can't fail. She love it!. Now... first, let her know I here. Easy. Throw...

Looks around for something to throw.

... this, (*Finds a missile. Looks up at Judy's bedroom*). This do it. 'specially if it hits her. Bound to notice me then. Punch... you a genious!

Hurls the missile like a grenade through the window and squats underneath the sill chuckling. Scream of pain from JUDY within

JUDY: I knew it! Knew it! Sit down for five minutes, settle me feet, grab a breather to myself and... knew it!

Loud clatter of object thrown down angrily

Peace. That's all I want. Bit of peace. (*Another clatter*) 'ere I am, quiet as a mouse, doin' me toilet, and you, *You* you lout, you 'ead-banger whoever you is, 'ave's to interrupt, break me concentration. An' you know what that means. Well, You've asked for it, you 'ave.

Emerges at the window carrying the missile, hideous anger. Leans out, searching

I'll bloody well show you whoever you are!
(*Looks looks around*)... wherever you are.

Looks down, notices PUNCH who is doubled up laughing, grins, holds the missile at arms length

You can 'ave it back.

Drops it, sees it crack PUNCH on the head and turns chuckling back into her room

PUNCH: (*Writhing in mock pain*) Aaaaaagh! What a mess what a mess.

JUDY heard laughing. PUNCH takes off his hat and reveals a very solid skull protector underneath. Begins a hideous chuckle. Loud. JUDY laughs.

She's in. Yes she is. I can tell. (*Rubs skull protector*) Instinct! (*Loud*) Oh... dear! (*Hoots of laughter from JUDY. To self*) Now then, what to do?

Sudden inspiration followed by the now familiar crack of the slapstick

Yeesss! Window open... (*Hideous chuckle*) she'll be able to hear my woo. So... (*Wooing posture*) Right (*Clears throat*) Errrrr... (*No other sound emerges. Sudden amnesia*) Start again. (*Same wooing posture*) Errrrr... (*Same problem of amnesia*) I know... (*Sudden inspiration*) I'll ask Judy. She'll know. That's it... (*Inspirational gesture*) Ask Judy. (*Prepares an 'ask Judy' posture*) Judy... (*Clears throat. Louder*) Judy... (*No response. Louder*) Judy... (*No response. Louder*) Judy Judy Judy... JUDY!

(*JUDY appears sudddenly at the window looking very threatening. PUNCH moves into her focus*) Judy Judy Judy...Judy!

JUDY: (*Squinting*) Who's that?
PUNCH: Judy...!
JUDY: (*More threatening*) Who's that?
PUNCH: Judy?!
JUDY: That's me. Who are you?
PUNCH: (*Stop messing about*) Judy...
JUDY: That's me as well.
PUNCH: (*Slightly desperate*) Judy?!
JUDY: If you say that again I'll throw something nasty at you. In fact...

Leans further out of the window for a closer look. Suspicions aroused

JUDY: Just a minute?
PUNCH: Yes?
JUDY: Are you the...
PUNCH: What?
JUDY: Are you the one who...
PUNCH: Me?
JUDY: You
PUNCH: (*Incredulous*) Me?!
JUDY: (*Grotesque smile of recognition*) Well I never.
PUNCH: You did!
JUDY: (*Arms akimbo*) Punch...
PUNCH: (*Points to his skull*) You did!
JUDY: (*Affectionately*) Punch...
PUNCH: Look (*More pointing*) This!

Picks up missile and mock hits himself using slapstick to produce the crack

This. You! (*Mock stagger*)
JUDY: (*Astounded*) Me?
PUNCH: You!
JUDY: That?

PUNCH: You!.
JUDY: Oh Punch Punchy Punchy
PUNCH: (*Mock hurt*) You never thought you would do this...
JUDY: Oh Punchy. Wouldn't have done that...
PUNCH: Never thought...
JUDY: Not me...
PUNCH: Not Judy...
JUDY: (*Pause. Smiling*) Punch... (*No response*) Punch... (*Shakes his head*) Punchie...? Shall I come down and make it better? (*No response*) Shall I? (*Slight flicker of interest*) Shall I... mend it. Shall I?
PUNCH: (*Mock petulant sulk*) No.
JUDY: (*Smiling*) Punch...?
PUNCH: (*Stamping foot*) No!
JUDY: (*Huge grin*) I'm coming (*She disappears*)
PUNCH: (*Huge grin*) Easy.

Presses a blood capsule – disguised as a grape – on his forehead, and begins the countdown to her appearance, at the same time preparing a grotesque posture of extreme pain. Covers eyes with hands

Seven, five, six...
JUDY: (*From without*) Nearly there.
PUNCH: Three...
JUDY: (*Closer*) Are you ready?
PUNCH: (*Another grotesque shudder*) Two...
JUDY: Close you eyes
PUNCH: (*Beside himself*) One...!
JUDY: (*Jumps behind Punch*) Here!
PUNCH: (*Uncovers eyes*) Where?
JUDY: Here!

She leaps onto his back, and covers his eyes with her hands. They go into a 'find each other' Lazzo, which concludes with JUDY trying desperately to place her feet on the ground. This is achieved only after much acrobatic contortion–a bit like the music-hall deck-chair routine–and an exchange of monosyllabic grunts. At the end of the Lazzo JUDY notices PUNCH'S bleeding skull. She starts laughing

JUDY: Oh Punchy, look at you, just look at you.
PUNCH: How?
JUDY: Eh?
PUNCH: How can I look at me?
JUDY: Easy?
PUNCH: How easy?
JUDY: In a mirror.

PUNCH: (*Smiling*) Easy. (*Smile fades*) Not easy.
JUDY: (*Still chuckling*) Easy.
PUNCH: No easy. No mirror.
JUDY: Yes.
PUNCH: No! No mirror!
JUDY: Yes, yes mirror. In my bedroom.
PUNCH: (*Grotesque realisation*) Eassssssssy (*Mock pain and staggering again*)
JUDY: (*Embracing PUNCH*) Let me mend it. Let me make it better. In my... bedroom. Come on Punchie (*Takes his arm*)
PUNCH: (*More staggering and mock resistance*) OOOoooooh no!
JUDY: Punch?
PUNCH: No!
JUDY: Please...
PUNCH: Couldn't...
JUDY: Go on...
PUNCH: Can't
JUDY: Go on...
PUNCH: Can't
JUDY: Why not... ?
PUNCH: Might hurt...
JUDY: I be ever so gentle...
PUNCH: You won't...
JUDY: Will...
PUNCH: Honest?
JUDY: Honest...
PUNCH: (*Hideous grin*) Allright then...

Allows himself to be led into Judy's bedroom. When he gets to the entrance he becomes mock reluctant

Promise?
JUDY: Course I be gentle. Always... gentle (*Quiet. Menacing*) Always quiet with Punchy. Always.

After a moment's thought. PUNCH suddenly brightens

PUNCH: O... K... (*Offers his head*)

During the ensuing sequence JUDY'S objective is to secure the slapstick... and use it!. A 'slapstick stealing' Lazzo ensues. She creates a series of 'distractions', by stroking different parts of PUNCH, in the hope that he will release his grip on the slapstick, and thus enable her to steal it

JUDY: (*Stroking his feet*) Where does it hurt?

PUNCH: (*Indicating his head*) There.
JUDY: (*Legs*) There?
PUNCH: (*Indicating his head*) There!
JUDY: (*Thigh*) Here?
PUNCH: Yes. No!! (*Points vigorously to his head*) Here!!.

JUDY continues with a quick journey around PUNCH'S body. Each stroke or touch having same the affect as a game of 'tickles' with PUNCH becoming frustrated and amused at the same time, sometimes showing his pleasure and at others giving short snaps with his slapstick.
   Eventually he becomes a gibbering lump of contortion and in a final act of frustration releases both hands from his slapstick and places them on his head.
   At this JUDY removes the slapstick and hides it behind her

JUDY: Where?
PUNCH: (*Removes hat and skull cap*) HERE!!
JUDY: Close your eyes then.
PUNCH: (*Recoils*) What?!
JUDY: (*Very calm now*) Must close your eyes if I'm going to mend it; make it better. Must.
PUNCH: Now, must?
JUDY: Must.
PUNCH: O... K!

Covering eyes with hat and skull protector

There.

JUDY begins stroking PUNCH's head from behind with slapstick

JUDY: There?
PUNCH: (*Laughing*) No
JUDY: (*Stroking*) There?
PUNCH: No yes. Noo noo yes (*Pleasurable sigh*) There, no, yes.
JUDY: (*Stroking*) There.
PUNCH: (*Very quiet*) oooooh. That's... ooooh yeees

Opens his eyes and is about to feel the stroking slapstick. JUDY removes it and hides it behind her

JUDY: You're spoiling it. Much better when you got your eyes closed.
PUNCH: O... K!

Covers his eyes as before

Just... (*Indicates the spot*)... there

Growing excitement. JUDY prepares her target as she strokes it

JUDY: How's that?

Mesmerised. Swaying with the movement

PUNCH: Beeeeoooootiful.

JUDY lifts the slapstick ready for the strike

Don't stop.

PUNCH uncovers his eyes and spins round. JUDY manages to conceal the slapstick

JUDY: Don't peep.
PUNCH: (*Instantly covering his eyes*) I Won't I Won't I Won't!
JUDY: Don't.
PUNCH: Won't.
JUDY: There (*Return to the stroking only this time she includes a measuring pattern for the 'strike'*) How's that?
PUNCH: Beeootiful.
JUDY: Still beeootiful?
PUNCH: Beeootiful.
JUDY: Right. (*Striking posture*)
PUNCH: Right
JUDY: One (*Lift off*)
PUNCH: Right.
JUDY: Two (*Lift off*) Still beeootiful?
PUNCH: Bccootiful...
JUDY: Three! (*Mighty blow with the slapstick*) Beeeooootiful!!
PUNCH: (*Recoiling*) Oooohhhh!
JUDY: (*Strikes again*) Beeeeeoooootiful!
PUNCH: Oooohhhh!!
JUDY: Beeeeeoooootiful!!!

JUDY is about to strike again when HIMSELF enters and her action is frozen in mid-strike. HIMSELF is dressed like a stereotypical countryman, plus-fours and deerstalker.

SCENE SIX

HIMSELF: Judy. What are you doing?!

PUNCH: (*Cowering. Anticipating blows*) Ohhhhhhh!
HIMSELF: Judy!
PUNCH: Judy! (*Very puzzled*) Who said that?
JUDY: (*Petrified*) You did.
PUNCH: I did?
JUDY: He did.
PUNCH: (*Grinning*) He did? Who did?
JUDY: (*Nodding in the direction of HIMSELF*) Er...
PUNCH: (*Mimicking, thinking a new game has begun*) Er...
HIMSELF: Me!

PUNCH sees HIMSELF at last. Stands. Self-preservation tactics immediately

PUNCH: You! (*Offers hand*) How do you do? Me...
HIMSELF: (*Ignoring*) Who are you?
PUNCH: I just going to tell...
HIMSELF: (*Turning to JUDY*) well?
PUNCH: Me...
HIMSELF: Judy?!
JUDY: (*Unscrambling*) 'Im. 'Ead. 'Is 'ead, very bad!

PUNCH takes the cue and sinks to his knees groaning

   Very bad. Smashed, in the street. Wicked it is...
PUNCH: Very very wicked...
JUDY: Very very wicked Sir Master yes...
HIMSELF: You mean to say that this... ?
JUDY: (*Almost together now*) In the street. Outside our front door. Saw it
   from my window...
PUNCH: (*Pointing to his head*) There
JUDY: Couldn't miss.
PUNCH: Yeh.
JUDY: There I was, in me room, doing me toilet...

PUNCH copies the odd word as he follows Judy's story and then joins in the improvised 'reconstruction'

PUNCH: Judy. Jooooooooody!
JUDY: Like a nightmare it was. In me toilet doing me room by the
   window bold as you like all of a sudden...
PUNCH: Judy, Joooooooooody!
JUDY: Just like that. Then out of nowhere as if by magic

She delivers three shattering blows with the slapstick to PUNCH'S head

Smash smash smash!

PUNCH drops like a stone, death rattles – the lot

Just like that. So I rush downstairs, open the door, and there, right in front of me, covered in blood...

PUNCH: *(Staggering)* Me.

JUDY: Like a rag doll.

PUNCH: Yeh me!

JUDY: Dead!

PUNCH: Me. Dead!

JUDY: *(Encouraging him)* Lying there.

PUNCH: *(Gormless)* Yeh

JUDY: Lying there.

PUNCH: Yeh

JUDY: *(JUDY whips his legs from beneath him)* Just like that.

PUNCH: Me.

JUDY: 'Orrible.

Pause.

HIMSELF: I'll ring for the Police.

PUNCH: Yeh.

JUDY: Yeh.

HIMSELF: Now. While the scent's still hot. Catch the yob. Or were there more of them?

PUNCH: Yeh.

JUDY: Seven

PUNCH: *(Brightly)* Yeh. *(Angry)* More

HIMSELF: Really?

JUDY: Ten.

HIMSELF: Ten?

PUNCH: *(Grinning)* Yeh

HIMSELF: Good God. A tribe!

PUNCH: *(Hideous)* Yeh!

HIMSELF: Police.

PUNCH: No!

HIMSELF: *(Insistent)* Police!

JUDY: No... Sir Master. No Police.

HIMSELF: Why ever not? This man has suffered. He's been brutally attacked and he's hurt.

PUNCH: *(Brightly)* Who is?

HIMSELF: You are.

PUNCH: I not.

HIMSELF: You were.

PUNCH: (*Standing threatening*) Not!
HIMSELF: I saw you.
PUNCH: Where?
HIMSELF: (*Indicating his head*) There.
PUNCH: (*Mock terror*) This? (*Points to head*) Me?
HIMSELF: You.
JUDY: (*Belts him*) Like that. You!

PUNCH sinks to his knees

HIMSELF: Police!

Decision made, turns to go. With amazing agility PUNCH and JUDY leap before him, threatening

PUNCH: No!
JUDY: No Police.
HIMSELF: Well, if you think so...
JUDY: We do. (*PUNCH flops groaning*)
HIMSELF: Then the least we can do is help this man Judy. (*Adopts political attitude*) We must care for him as though he were one of our own; on the same side of the road.
PUNCH: (*Mock overwhelmed*) Very kind. You very kind very very indeed very kind.
HIMSELF: (*Suitably flattered*) Not at all. Least we could do. Now Judy. I think we ought to dress his wounds don't you? Mm?
PUNCH: (*Mock pathetic*) I OK. This hat... enough.
HIMSELF: Won't hear of it. Bandages Judy. Bandages and water. Quickly now!

PUNCH goes into a mock feint. Himself catches him and helps him to a seat. JUDY exits helpless with laughter

SCENE SEVEN

HIMSELF: You are a very brave young man.
PUNCH: Yeh.
HIMSELF: Unbelievable courage.
PUNCH: Yeh.
HIMSELF: I need someone like you.
PUNCH: Yeh.
HIMSELF: Wouldn't be interested would you...?
PUNCH: (*Switched off*) Yeh
HIMSELF: In a job...?
PUNCH: Yeh.

HIMSELF: For me...?
PUNCH: Yeh.
HIMSELF: As a gardener...?
PUNCH: Yeh.
HIMSELF: Work, for me, as a gardener?
PUNCH: Yeh (*Double take*) Work?!!
HIMSELF: Yes.
PUNCH: 'Work' work?!!
HIMSELF: As my gardener.
PUNCH: (*Flops*) Oh...
HIMSELF: Problems?
PUNCH: I have to think about it.
HIMSELF: Of course...
PUNCH: Very busy at the now.

Goes into an instant flurry of meaningless activity

HIMSELF: Quite.
PUNCH: Quite.
HIMSELF: Must be difficult.
PUNCH: But...
HIMSELF: Yes?
PUNCH: I been always want an interview. Never had one.
HIMSELF: Aha!
PUNCH: Can I'ave one?
HIMSELF: How about tomorrow, say four o'clock?
PUNCH: I say anything you like if I have an interview. Four o'clock, four
    o'clock, four o'clock...

JUDY returns with huge rolls of bandage.

HIMSELF: Aha!
PUNCH: (*Collapsing in a heap*) Ahhhhhh!
HIMSELF: Do you mind if I leave you?
PUNCH: (*Instantly better*) Yes!
HIMSELF: Blood you see. Can't stand the sight of it. So... tomorrow at
    four. Er... you're in good hands. Good, good... (*Moves briskly out*) Good.

SCENE EIGHT

*JUDY is very excited at the thought of immobilising PUNCH and giving him
a real thrashing. She is measuring out lengths of bandage between outstretched
arms.*

JUDY: That'll do.
PUNCH: Is it?
JUDY: Let's start with your (*Attacking PUNCH with bandage*)... head!
PUNCH: (*Dodging*) I going.

JUDY bars his exit with a length of bandage

JUDY: No way.
PUNCH: Oh Judy Judy, I need kip. Interview tomorrow. Job, money...
JUDY: Don't soft-soap me.
PUNCH: Me?!
JUDY: That 'ead, these bandages, mend. Me!
PUNCH: Judy... ?
JUDY: Now!
PUNCH: Now?
JUDY: NOW?
PUNCH: O... K. (*Judy relaxes*) But... (*JUDY tenses again*) Please be gentle.
JUDY: (*Mock caring*) Oh Punch. Poor poor Punchy.

Moves seat to the centre of the room and nods to PUNCH indicating that he sits

PUNCH: (*Mimicking the nod without sitting*) Right.
JUDY: (*Nods*) Right.
PUNCH: (*Mimics*) Right.
JUDY: (*Angry*) There!
PUNCH: (*Mimicking*) There!

JUDY spits with anger reducing the length of bandage by winding it over each fist

JUDY: Now! There! Chair! There! Now!

PUNCH contemplates mimicking this lot but thinks better of it and goes 'tired' like a badly thrown pot. Strokes the chair like a cat

PUNCH: There there. (*Sits*) There.

JUDY moves behind him as though she is about to garrotte him. PUNCH senses this and slides down the chair snatching his slapstick from JUDY's waistband. He stands very tall, slapstick raised as though he is going to decapitate JUDY. Softens slightly, and turns his attention to his slapstick and away from the cowering JUDY

There there. Lovely stick, lovely stick. Did you miss me then? (*Feels his head*) Don't think so.

Smiles again and strokes the chair with the slapstick

Nice chair. Nicey nicey. There there

Whacks the chair and then sits on it quickly as though he is sitting on his victim. Slapstick held like an erect phallus

Judy, make me better...
JUDY: (*Lowering bandage*) No.
PUNCH: Now!
JUDY: No.
PUNCH: (*Testing*) Judy?
JUDY: No!
PUNCH: (*Lowering slapstick*) Judy? Head. Aches.
JUDY: Good!
PUNCH: Sore.
JUDY: Serves you right.
PUNCH: Judy?
JUDY: Go away.
PUNCH: Judy?
JUDY: Or I'll scream.
PUNCH: (*Pleading. Soft*) Judy?
JUDY: (*Threatening*) I will!
PUNCH: (*Sitting down*) I only came for a woo. My head sore. Make it better.?
JUDY: You mean it?
PUNCH: (*Ugly grin*) Mean it. Make it better then I'll...
JUDY: Yes?
PUNCH: Woo you!
JUDY: (*Very bright*) You will?
PUNCH: Yeh.
JUDY: Woo?
PUNCH: Woo.
JUDY: OOOOoooooo! (*Tries to remove slapstick*) You won't need that.
PUNCH: (*Grinning*) Will!
JUDY: Please yourself. Now... where does it hurt?

Both go into a 'where does it hurt' Lazzo

In the next sequence PUNCH ends up being mummified, arms slung back like a straightjacket leaving the slapstick easy to remove

JUDY: Now then. Let's see. Make a sling.
PUNCH: Wha?

JUDY: Everyone'll feel sorry for you if you 'ave a sling.
PUNCH: I have two slings!
JUDY: There. Better?
PUNCH: Yeh. Liked that. Head?
JUDY: Leave that 'till last.
PUNCH: (*Lunatic grin*) Yeh!
JUDY: Now, your feet.
PUNCH: Feets? Why you what to mend feets for? It my 'ands and...'ead...

Realises that he can't touch his hands or his head because they are immobilised

JUDY: (*Already attacking his feet*) Got to.
PUNCH: Eh?
JUDY: Mended your 'ands, right?
PUNCH: Yeh.
JUDY: Feels better, right?
PUNCH: Yeh.
JUDY: Then...
PUNCH: Feets. (*Another lunatic grin*) Yesssss.
JUDY: (*Tying off feet to chair*) Better?
PUNCH: Yeh. How I look?
JUDY: Very smashing!
PUNCH: What next?
JUDY: Best bit.
PUNCH: (*Huge chuckle*) Best bit?
JUDY: Yeh.
PUNCH: Wassat?
JUDY: (*Indicates head*) Best bit.
PUNCH: (*Huge lunatic grin*) Yeh!

Looks around his body, realises his predicament, and begins to laugh

JUDY: (*Joining in the laughter*) What you laughing at?
PUNCH: You!

JUDY removes the slapstick with great deliberation from PUNCH'S hands without his being aware

JUDY: Me?
PUNCH: You!

JUDY cracks him over the head with the slapstick

JUDY: Me?!

PUNCH: (*Instantly devastated*) Me.
JUDY: Good. I'm laughing at you too.
PUNCH: We both laughing at me too. (*Wearily*) All I want is to woo you
   Judy.
JUDY: Yeh.
PUNCH: (*Very quiet*) I think I going to scream.
JUDY: (*Equally quiet*) You?
PUNCH: Me.

JUDY moves behind him, slapstick raised

JUDY: you?
PUNCH: (*Loud*) I. YES! (*Shouting*) ME!!

*JUDY places slapstick carefully in PUNCH'S lap, then curtails his screaming
by gagging PUNCH with the bandage*

JUDY: No. (*Quietly. Sinister*) No scream.

*Begins winding bandage about the head of PUNCH, his nose, ears, leaving the
eyes*

No scream, no smell, no hear.

Finishes off around head

You hear me?

PUNCH shakes his head, JUDY winds more around his ears

Now? (*Shakes his head. JUDY winds more around his ears*) Now? (*PUNCH
shakes his head. Another wind*) Now? (*No reaction*) Breath? (*No response*)
Can (*Mouthing*) can, you, breath? (*No response*)

Good. You dead!!! For the mo' that will do. You better now.

*Ties off final bandage. Picks up slapstick and stands behind PUNCH resting
the slapstick on PUNCH'S head gently tapping to punctuate the ensuing
dialogue*

Poor... Punch (*He closes his eyes wincing*) Better now. Whack you as
much as I like now. You dead (*PUNCH opens his eyes appealingly*) You
not dead (*Punch winces*) Oh dear. Oh deary deary me. Poor Punch. Let
me make it better. Poor poorly Punch. Who's a clever boy then? There

there, there there. Better? Better Punchy. Look at me punchy Lovely Punch look at Judy. Punch?

Getting irritated. 'Taps' getting stronger

Punch? You *not* dead Punch I *know* you not dead. Not yet. So... (*PUNCH'S head lolls forward*) Oh dear.

Lifts and lowers head with the end of the slapstick

JUDY: Up and down, up and down. Up up up, and down. You better now Punchy? Head better, Punchy? (*Pauses*) You dead again Punchy? (*No response*) Punchy? (*PUNCH nods slowly*) You better? (*nods*) you really better? (*PUNCH nods wearily*) Oh... Punchy

Drops slapstick and gives him a huge hug sitting astride his knees

I think you ready for your woo aren't you.

Punch lowers his head into her breast

A good woo, you really do.

She gets off, and begins pulling at the final loose end of the bandaging. As she pulls PUNCH stands up and begins spinning as the bandage unravels until he spins off stage, with JUDY following the trail of bandage

SCENE NINE – The Great House

A solitary chair. HIMSELF and HERSELF moving with the slight suggestion of peacock and hen, HIMSELF is wrestling with a problem, HERSELF awaits the answer. The pattern of movement should reflect this.

HERSELF: Well?
HIMSELF: I'm not sure
HERSELF: I don't believe it.
HIMSELF: What do you expect?
HERSELF: Something!
HIMSELF: I see. (*Rhetorical pose*) Well now...
HIMSELF: (*Instant boredom*) Yes?
HIMSELF: It's not easy.
HERSELF: It never is.
HIMSELF: I mean, I thought I'd got it all sewn up?
HERSELF: Wish you had.

HIMSELF: Meaning?

HERSELF: Why bother me? *Your* decision.

HIMSELF: But it affects *you* as well darling.

HERSELF: Affects *Judy, not* me!

HIMSELF: But Judy's *your* housekeeper, *your* nanny.

HERSELF: *Our!*

HIMSELF: What?

HERSELF: *Our* housekeeper, *our* nanny. She looks after *us* and *it*.!

HIMSELF: It?

HERSELF: *Our it!*

HIMSELF: Oh *him*...

HERSELF: Quite...

HIMSELF: I see.

HERSELF: Nothing to do with me! (*Sits*) Nothing! Do what you like, feed another mouth. I care not!

HIMSELF: (*Brighter*) Don't you really?

HERSELF: (*Standing angrily*) I'm going to bed!

HIMSELF: But it's the middle of the afternoon. You've just got up.

HERSELF: This has made me tired and it's too bright. You know how I hate the sun!

HIMSELF: Of course, how silly of me. Sorry darling. Well I'd better get on with it. He's waiting outside. Wish me luck.

HERSELF: (*Ignoring him*) I'll bring 'it' in after an hour, with some tea. See how *he* reacts to 'it'. But don't you dare do anything which will upset Judy. She's irreplaceable. Don't want her producing her 'it' before *our* 'it' has flown the nest. That's what worries me...

HIMSELF: Quite!

HERSELF: Quite!

PUNCH mimicking 'quite' from without

You look tired. (*Kisses him dispassionately*) I'll send him in.

HERSELF sweeps out. PUNCH mimics 'quite' as HERSELF shouts 'in' as she passes. HIMSELF sinks wearily into the chair closing his eyes uttering a deep sigh

SCENE TEN – The Great House, as before

PUNCH enters with a large bloodstained bandage around his hat. He is eating cherries, he wipes his fingers on his bandage adding to the effect of the bloodstains. He is grinning hideously. An 'interview' grin.

PUNCH: Hello. (*No response*) Quite. (*Steps closer*) Quite. Hello quite? (*No reply*) Can I hear me? (*Shouts*) Hellooooooo? (*No response*) Quite. You asleep. Master asleep. You asleep then I asleep. You want me to do it. I do it I sleep. O.K? O.K. I sleep. (*Stands like an owl dozing*) Twit to woooo. Twit to woooo. I asleep so are youoooo.

HIMSELF wakes suddenly as if from a nightmare. Sees PUNCH. Instant 'interview' attitude

Er... sit down will you?
PUNCH: Can't.
HIMSELF: Please

Indicating that he sits in a chair which isn't there

PUNCH: Can't.
HIMSELF: Why not?
PUNCH: I asleep.
HIMSELF: Tired?
PUNCH: No.
HIMSELF: Head?
PUNCH: No.
HIMSELF: What then?
PUNCH: Asleep! (*Head lolls*) Twit to woooo...
HIMSELF: (*Suddenly standing*) Good! Now then (*Proffers a handshake*) How do you do?

PUNCH becomes instantly awake. Takes HIMSELF'S hand and shakes it without releasing it

PUNCH: Twit to woooo, very please to eat you.

HIMSELF takes PUNCH on a stroll still holding the handshake

HIMSELF: Good.
PUNCH: Yeh.
HIMSELF: Nervous?
PUNCH: Me?
HIMSELF: Mm.
PUNCH: No. (*They stop*) You?
HIMSELF: Good Lord no!
PUNCH: Then we both not nervous. Please.

Extends free hand to indicate chair

Please

Releases handshake

HIMSELF: *(Sitting)* Thank you. Very kind.

Pause. Still.

You shake well.
PUNCH: Yeh.
HIMSELF: Dry...
PUNCH: Yeh.
HIMSELF: Firm...
PUNCH: Yeh.
HIMSELF: Gardener's hands.
PUNCH: Yeh. How much?

Stretches out his hands about waist width

HIMSELF: About ten acres.

PUNCH stretches his hands and arms wide apart. Incredulous

PUNCH: How much is that?
HIMSELF: Enough.
PUNCH: *(Drops his hands)* Yeh.
HIMSELF: *(Standing)* Please. *(Indicates that PUNCH should sit. He does so)* Judy...
PUNCH: *(Happy growl)* No. Punch. Dooty dooty do.
HIMSELF: You misunderstand. You and Judy? You er...

PUNCH begins mimicking from his seat the attitudes adopted by HIMSELF as he pontificates

PUNCH: Yeh?
HIMSELF: It's not just a matter of the garden, it's more a matter of looking ahead. The future. Time passing. A sense of permanence. You see... in this household we like to maintain a feeling of family. A kind of family... feeling. Master and Mistress, Judy and Punch and... 'it'.
PUNCH: Eh?
HIMSELF: 'It'!
PUNCH: Thank you.
HIMSELF: Quite. Judy looks after us and it. Don't want to upset the balance, tip the fulcrum so to speak. So... ?
PUNCH: Yeh?

HIMSELF: So... ?
PUNCH: So... ?
HIMSELF: You accept?
PUNCH: (*Hideous grin*) No.
HIMSELF: Why ever not?
PUNCH: (*Instant serious*) I worried. About *work*.
HIMSELF: A gardener has to work. *Big* garden, lots of *work*.
PUNCH: Lot and lots of work?
HIMSELF: Noo... just *lots* of work.
PUNCH: Oh. That allright then.
HIMSELF: Quite. Now...
PUNCH: (*Very strong*) I, like to live with Judy. Without Judy I very sad, very lonely. Big droop. Big, big droop.
HIMSELF: What you're saying is that...
PUNCH: Yes!

Pause. Still

HIMSELF: In that case, no problem.
PUNCH: I fetch my tool.
HIMSELF: You brought them with you?
PUNCH: No.
HIMSELF: Marvellous. (*Enter HERSELF carrying 'it'*) Aha!

SCENE ELEVEN – (*Continuing*)

PUNCH: (*Mimicking*) Aha!

Sees baby. Instant glee. Begins to finger slapstick

PUNCH: Oooooh. Dooty dooooo...
HERSELF: Tea?
PUNCH: (*Mock shy*) Yeh.
HERSELF: Darling?
PUNCH: Yeh.

Can't take his eyes off HERSELF and the BABY

HERSELF: (*Ignoring this*) Be here in a tick darling.
HIMSELF: Er... Mr Punch I think darling, unless I misunderstood which I don't think I did unless I'm absolutely mistaken... has agreed to...
HERSELF: Really? (*Hands BABY to HIMSELF*) I think I'm going to be sick!

HIMSELF catches the smell and hands IT back instantly

Ugh, no. Can't. It might...

HERSELF: It has! That's while I feel sick. If you don't take it I'll drop it. I shan't be responsible.

PUNCH, hovering excitedly like a paragon of parenthood opens his arms

Me. Give to me. I look after lovely baby.

Takes baby with consummate care

Now you can be sick.

Begins rocking baby from side to side. Cooing hideously

Lovely baby, lovely baby who's a lovely baby then? Who's a lovely baby. Mummy's going to be sick, and Daddy doesn't like your dooty doo so I look after you. (*Starts singing*) Cutchie cutchie cutchie coo. Rock-a-bye, rock-a-bye. Dooty dooty dooty do, Mummy's going to be sick! (*BABY begins to whimper*)

HERSELF: Not!

PUNCH: Mummy's *not* going to be sick.

Swinging a slightly bigger arc now. BABY beginning to cry. JUDY produces the 'cry' from the chorus

Rock-a-bye, rock-a-bye, baby...

HIMSELF: I'm *very* impressed. Looks as though you've done that before.

PUNCH: (*Totally flipped*) Mummy's better, rock-a-bye, rock-a-bye... (*BABY crying in earnest now*)

HERSELF: (*Slightly alarmed*) Much better now. Think I can manage. (*Attempts to remove BABY from PUNCH*) Very kind of you...

PUNCH: (*Totally ignoring her*) Rock-a-bye up and down, rock-a-bye up and down...

HERSELF: I'll take it now. Thank you very much. Thank you...

PUNCH: Up and down, go to sleep, up and down (*High swings now. Baby screaming*)

HERSELF is trying desperately to catch one of the downward swings now

HERSELF: Thank you, VERY much...

PUNCH is now swinging the baby by its legs like a swingboat

PUNCH: Lovely baby, baby crying, naughty baby, naughty baby, shut you mouth you squawling brat, pussy cat, stinky shat...

HERSELF: (*At a total loss*) I think baby's had enough 'cuddling' now. Don't want to spoil it do we Mr... er? I'm truly very grateful. Thank you *very* much... you're very *very* sweet...
HIMSELF: I think he knows what he's doing darling...
HERSELF: Don't think so darling
HIMSELF: Does darling
PUNCH: Naughty baby naughty baby stop crying stop it stop it stop it!

Slapstick 'drawn' ready for a swipe as baby is tossed into the air. HERSELF grabs the baby just before the horrific blow and rushes off. PUNCH trembles with rage

HIMSELF: (*To no one in particular*) There we are what did I tell you? Mr Punch our new gardener is happy with children. One of the family already. *Very* impressive. You are most welcome. When can you start?
PUNCH: (*Slapstick swinging, still threatening*) Naughty baby...
HIMSELF: Tomorrow? Tomorrow convenient?
PUNCH: Naughty!
HIMSELF: Good.
PUNCH: Bad!
HIMSELF: See you tomorrow then. Take you round the garden. Ten thirty soon enough?
PUNCH: Naughty baby!
HIMSELF: Good. I'm sure you'll be very happy...
PUNCH: (*Turning towards HIMSELF slowly*) Very naughty ... !

HIMSELF exits humming contentedly. PUNCH slowly relaxes and transports us to ...

SCENE TWELVE – The Garden

The following morning. PUNCH dons his gardening clothes – wellies, waistcoat, cap, everything stereotypical you can think of – establishes a bench and pots and begins breaking them with his slapstick, with relish. HIMSELF enters, hears the happy sound of work in progress and grins.

HIMSELF: Aha!

PUNCH is totally absorbed in joyful destruction

PUNCH: Smash smash smash! (*Does so. Picks up new pot*) Samash! (*Does so*) Samash! (*Does so*) Samash! Smashing!

Stamps feet on pile of broken pots to crush the bits

22. Punch

23. Himself

Smash smash smash...

As he stamps he notices HIMSELF'S feet amidst the debris. Bends down to take a closer look

Where they come from?

About to smash them with slapstick when they move, HIMSELF rocking on his heels. PUNCH leaps back and lets his eyes travel up the body, until he is standing face to face with HIMSELF. PUNCH becomes instantly servile

HIMSELF: Morning.
PUNCH: Morning.
HIMSELF: Busy?
PUNCH: Yeh.
HIMSELF: Good.
PUNCH: Morning.
HIMSELF: Very good morning. Lovely day. Everything allright?
PUNCH: Yeh.
HIMSELF: Good, good. Er... what are you doing?
PUNCH: (*Smashing a pot*) Smashing!
HIMSELF: So I see.
PUNCH: Smashing morning.
HIMSELF: Oh... yes. Going to last don't y'think?

Looks at the destruction before him. With extreme tact

Er... (*Nods in the direction of the debris*)

PUNCH: Crocks.
HIMSELF: And?
PUNCH: Drainage.
HIMSELF: Aha (*Shallow smile*) To place in the... (*Mimes this*) bottom of the... er... (*Looks around in vain for an unsmashed pot*) Have we *any*?
PUNCH: (*Hideous grin*) No.
HIMSELF: (*Sickly grin*) Aha.
PUNCH: Need some new ones.
HIMSELF: (*Sifting a pile of wreckage with his foot*) These... er... past it?
PUNCH: (*Instantly aggressive*) Yessss!

HIMSELF begins carefully, growing in confidence

HIMSELF: You broke the er... pots, the er... terracotta pots... er... that er ... *which* we've had in this family for more than thirty years – since I was a young man in fact – even though they were still serviceable... Mmm?
PUNCH: (*Aggressive*) Mmmm! Yessss!
HIMSELF: (*Totally squashed*) Good. New broom...
PUNCH: Smash pots!
HIMSELF: Quite. A clean start.
PUNCH: A *smashing* start!
HIMSELF: Quite! Now...

PUNCH confronts with much chin-jutting

PUNCH: Yessss?!
HIMSELF: (*Backing off*) How about a tour of the garden before...
PUNCH: I smash more pots! .
HIMSELF: No... before morning tea break.
PUNCH: (*Instantly placated. Grinning*) Ohhh yeh!
HIMSELF: Well... (*Leading Punch*) Shall we begin with the Berberis. Berberis Choisya Ternata, from Mexico. Lovely fragrance, beautiful white flowers... You will no doubt be familiar with...
PUNCH: Yeh.

They go for a stroll around the garden

SCENE THIRTEEN – The Kitchen as before

JUDY enters twisting sausages. Washing in progress, piles of washing sorted on the floor, radio blaring close to the squawling 'it'. Enter HERSELF unseen

24. Herself

by JUDY. *She scans the chaos and tries in vain to attract JUDY'S attention. Eventually switches off the radio. The baby screaming.*

JUDY: (*Still not seeing HERSELF*) You little sod! You scheming little sod!

Scuttles to 'it' with her hands outstretched spanned with a length of sausage as though to garrotte. She stops when she sees HERSELF

JUDY: Morning Mistress.
HERSELF: Morning Judy. Er...
JUDY: (*Dropping the sausages*) The little love. 'E's tired. Ready for 'is kip bless 'im. I'll take 'im outside bless 'im. Won't be a sec. (*Does so and returns*) Bless 'im. Sorry about that. Got a lot on. (*Back to sausages*)
HERSELF: (*Mock sympathetic*) I can see that.
JUDY: Never seems to stop. 'Scuse me.

Scuttles to the washing machine, tears out washed clothes and stuffs in a pile of dirty ones. Back to the sausages

Lovely morning.
HERSELF: Yes. I wonder if we could...
JUDY: (*Heavy sarcasm*) Be with you in a minute Miss. Won't be long.
HERSELF: I wonder if it's possible Judy...

JUDY: Everything's possible Miss, especially *this* morning when there's not much to do.

HERSELF: In that case would you mind leaving it just for a moment and...

JUDY: What?!

HERSELF: (*Very emphatic*) Just for a moment. I want to...!

JUDY drops the sausages where she is standing, switches off the washing machine, scuttles outside to silence the squawling baby, and rushes back to HERSELF, her hands still twisting sausages

JUDY: Yeh? what is it? Out with it. What d'you want? 'Aven't got all day!

JUDY bursts into false laughter as though she was joking

HERSELF: (*Very still*) Would you mind sitting down?

JUDY: (*Laughing*) I'd rather not. Might effect me rhythm. (*Hands and body all action*)

HERSELF: Very well (*Sits*) The gardener, our *new* gardener, *your* friend. I'm a little worried...

JUDY stops twisting. Thrusts hands into the pockets of her apron. Short burst of movement and then still

JUDY: Yes?!

HERSELF: I'm worried.

JUDY: So am I.

HERSELF: Oh?

JUDY: Not like 'im...

HERSELF: Really?

JUDY: Work.

HERSELF: Yes?

JUDY: Never done it before.

HERSELF: No Judy. Wrong tack altogether. Nothing to do with work. I know nothing about *work* Judy. It's... well... you.

JUDY: Me?

HERSELF: You.

JUDY: (*Very defensive*) Me?! Nothing wrong with *my* work is there?

HERSELF: Good Lord no! You must never think that Judy, never. It's him, the gardener... possibilities.

JUDY: Don't get you.

HERSELF: Relationships. *You* and *him*. Permanent!

JUDY: No.

HERSELF: No?

JUDY: No!

HERSELF: Really? Well (*Begins to stand, smiling*) In that case...
JUDY: Not yet!
HERSELF: (*Sitting hard*) Really? When?!
JUDY: When I'm ready.
HERSELF: I see. So you are *thinking* of... ?
JUDY: I've thought. I am!
HERSELF: Oh...
JUDY: (*Suddenly springing to life*) I'll 'ave to get on. (*Back to the sausages*)
HERSELF: Oh! Right! Erm... what are these for?
JUDY: Eating. Tea!
HERSELF: 'Course. Silly of me.
JUDY: Yes.
HERSELF: See you at lunch.
JUDY: Right.
HERSELF: One o'clock be allright?
JUDY: Right!

HERSELF glides thoughtfully out

SCENE FOURTEEN – Another Part of the Garden

PUNCH and HIMSELF are continuing their tour. HIMSELF is philosophising.

HIMSELF: I'd be much happier. None of the pressures I have now. You see, I inherited this...

Wide gesture which includes the 'grand design'. Stops and focuses upon a rose cradling it in his hand. This could be a pom pom on PUNCH's shoe or hat

Look at that...
PUNCH: Yeh.
HIMSELF: Isn't that the most exquisite red rose you've ever seen?
PUNCH: Yeh.
HIMSELF: 'Papa Meilland' Amazing how it's survived in this dreadful bed.
PUNCH: Yeh.
HIMSELF: You agree?
PUNCH: Yeh.
HIMSELF: (*Laughing*) Excellent. I love philosophising don't you?
PUNCH: Love it.
HERSELF: Here we are, you and me...
PUNCH: Me and you...
HIMSELF: You to the left

PUNCH is puzzled at this because he is standing on the right of HIMSELF

PUNCH: Yeh.
HIMSELF: Me to the right...

PUNCH begins to take note now, mimicking the indication to right and left

PUNCH: You to the right... no, you on my *left*...
HIMSELF: The political and social spectrum represented by the two extremes, Right and Left...

PUNCH begins pirouetting with the problem of 'right' and 'left'

PUNCH: Left right right left left right... Yeh?
HIMSELF: And we share the same garden...
PUNCH: Yeh.
HIMSELF: Philosophising...
PUNCH: Yeh!
HIMSELF: Wish I was gardener like you.
PUNCH: Wish you was a gardener like me.
HIMSELF: Quite.
PUNCH: (*Chuckle*) Quite.
HIMSELF: Quite.
PUNCH: You can.
HIMSELF: Pardon?
PUNCH: Be one.
HIMSELF: What?
PUNCH: Be a 'what', a gardener.
HIMSELF: How can I possibly be a gardener?
PUNCH: Easy.
HIMSELF: How?
PUNCH: Be one. Have my job. Be a gardener. (*Getting very excited*) *You* be me. *You* be *my* gardener.
HIMSELF: *Your* gardener?
PUNCH: Yeh. You be me an' I be you. Then we both happy cos... I *hate* this Pheasant job! I *hate* work! I like doing nothings! Like you, nothings! I like doing nothing like gardening. Gardening is the worst Pheasant job anyone can doing! So... *you* be gardener *me*, and I be Master, *you*! I *love* being *you*! Ohhhhhhh yes. Love it love it love it be you.
HIMSELF: Hadn't thought of that I must admit. It's a bit sudden. You seemed so...
PUNCH: Me?! In garden?! working?!! All that...

*PUNCH goes into an instant mimed compilation of gardening activities...
digging hoeing, raking etc*

HIMSELF: Yes?
PUNCH: And...

Continues mowing, hedging, strimming etc

HIMSELF: Yes?
PUNCH: *'Orrible*!! Pheasant'orrible work!!
HIMSELF: Aha! (*Sudden realisation*) You don't like it?
PUNCH: (*Huge grin*) No...
HIMSELF: Well well...
PUNCH: I very well...
HIMSELF: Correct me if I'm wrong...
PUNCH: You wrong...
HIMSELF: What you're saying is...
PUNCH: I right,
HIMSELF: *You, me,* for ever...
PUNCH: Yeh.
HIMSELF: Yes?
PUNCH: Yeh.
HIMSELF: (*Nodding*) Mmm...
PUNCH: (*Taking this as being an agreement*) Really? Shake hands really?
HIMSELF: (*Seduced into offering hand*) Yes.
PUNCH: I feel sick! Sick with happy. When... ?
HIMSELF: Now!
PUNCH: Now? You me me you shake hands really... now?
HIMSELF: Now.

*PUNCH continues shaking hands and taking off wellies and undoing
HIMSELF'S shoes at the same time*

PUNCH: You not change mind?
HIMSELF: No. I'm very happy.

*PUNCH continues muttering as he exchanges clothes with HIMSELF.
A 'metamorphosis' Lazzo which is mainly orchestrated by PUNCH. As each
dons the others' garments they both seem to take on the attitudes of their
adopted role*

PUNCH: If you happy then I happy. I very happy that you happy cos
you happy that I happy that you happy and if you happy that I happy
that I happy cos you happy that you happy then...

Once clothed, PUNCH draws himself up and begins to strut

And a now, I go for some tea. Teaeeeeeeee. You. A you pheasant off and go for some work! Me... tea. You... work! Now! Go! I very happy. Quite!

PUNCH struts off saying 'quite' often, whilst HIMSELF scuttles away happily

HIMSELF: Yeh!

SCENE FIFTEEN – The Dining Room of the Great House

JUDY is rushing to and fro setting the table for lunch.

HERSELF: (*Entering briskly*) Judy? (*Sees her*) Ah, Judy...

JUDY remains preoccupied with the task at hand

JUDY: Nearly there...

Blows a hunting horn, the signal for lunch.

HERSELF: I know that Judy but...

JUDY scuttles past HERSELF

JUDY: Just the spuds then we're ready.

Blows the horn again, moves off, blows another blast and returns with a final tureen

HERSELF: Marvellous, but where's the Master?
JUDY: Dunno.

Places the tureen in the centre of the table

'Aven't a clue.

Quick final check and stands in waiting' at the end of the table

Done my bit. Ready!
HERSELF: Wonderful Judy but where is he?
JUDY: 'Aven't seen 'im all morning 'aven't 'eard a squeak from 'is study a real puzzle I'm sure 'e'll be 'ere in a mo'.

HERSELF: *Very* strange!

Sits down on the seat to the left of the carver

Never late.
JUDY: Is!
HERSELF: Never.
JUDY: Today.
HERSELF: Today?
JUDY: Late, now, late!
HERSELF: (*Patronisingly*) But never before Judy.

JUDY is about to reply but stops at the entrance of PUNCH disguised as HIMSELF, looking every inch the part

Ah there you darling, thought we'd lost you. (*Gives him a peck*) Mmmm. (*PUNCH shudders with pleasure, HERSELF notices*) You all right? Not a chill I hope darling, you're unbearable when you've got a chill.
PUNCH: No. (*Very still*) Better now.
HERSELF: Thank God for that.

Sits at the table and shakes out her napkin. PUNCH copies this and throws his into one of the tureens opposite and sits opposite HERSELF and not at the head of the table

Darling... why are you sitting there?

JUDY removes the offending napkin and scuttles away looking back at PUNCH, puzzled

I repeat... why are *you* sitting *there*?

She indicates his usual place, the vacant carver

PUNCH: Because... (*Stands up uncertainly*) I am! (*Sits down in the same chair*) I am!
HERSELF: I can see that, but *why*?
PUNCH: Because... (*Sits in the carver chair*) I was...
HERSELF: Yes?
PUNCH: I want to play.
HERSELF: Play?!
PUNCH: Want to.
HERSELF: What?
PUNCH: (*Idiot grin*) Footsie

HERSELF: What?!
PUNCH: With you (*Begins stroking her leg with his outstretched foot*)
HERSELF: (*Horrified*) What are you doing?
PUNCH: Footsie
HERSELF: Will you stop it!
PUNCH: Shan't won't like it love it want to... (*Even more idiotic grin*)
HERSELF: What's got into you? Leave... (*Kicks foot away*) me (*Kicks again*) alone! (*Pushes her chair back*)
PUNCH: (*Ducking under the table undeterred*) Oooh yes look at that, oh yesss... (*Starts stroking her leg*)
HERSELF: Ahhhh...

JUDY enters and immediately notices the absence of HIMSELF

JUDY: Where's 'e gone now?

HERSELF trying desperately not to draw attention to the 'under-table' activity

HERSELF: Gone?
JUDY: Master. Gone. Do you want me to put 'is food back in the oven to keep warm?
HERSELF: I think he...
PUNCH: (*From below the table*) I here... Whorrr!

JUDY follows the distracting gaze of HERSELF as she looks to another part of the room

JUDY: Who said that?

PUNCH'S hand now visible above HERSELF'S knee

PUNCH: Meee!

HERSELF screams. JUDY moves backwards whence she has come, stifling a grin

JUDY: sorry... er... I'll... er... just go out. (*She does*)
HERSELF: (*Releasing a vicious kick at PUNCH*) You pig! You filthy imbecilic pig. You moron you

Kicks him again. PUNCH howls with pain

You're disgusting... ! (*Rushes out*)

SCENE SIXTEEN–(*Continuing*)

PUNCH eventually emerges groaning until he sees that he is alone and then breaks into a stream of laughter. He flops into the carver seat and suddenly notices the food and stops all sound, all movement

PUNCH: Look at that. Look at look at look at that. All that... look...

Dips finger into the nearest tureen, tastes it and growls with pleasure. Examines and dips into the others in turn.
A 'tasting Lazzo *ensues.*
Enter JUDY, *warily. She sidles up to her place and stands glancing at* PUNCH *disbelieving, stifling sniggers*
PUNCH *suddenly stops and looks directly at* JUDY *who continues sniggering until she realises that* PUNCH *is looking at her, she begins her 'twisting sausages' movement with her hands. He is like a dog with a bone*

JUDY: Er... can I?

Nods, indicating she wishes to sit. PUNCH *mimics her nodding.* JUDY *remains standing, totally thrown by this*

Is it all right? (*Nods again. More twitching*)
PUNCH: (*Thinking it is a game. More nodding and twitching*) What you do that for?
JUDY: What? (*Huge nod and twitch*)
PUNCH: (*Mimicking*) That. (*Another mimic*) This...
JUDY: You make me nervous Sir.
PUNCH: Me?
JUDY: (*In a fluster*) Shall I fetch the Mistress?
PUNCH: No. You sit and eat!
JUDY: Thank you sir.
PUNCH: Help yourself.
JUDY: After you Sir.
PUNCH: No...
JUDY: Sir?
PUNCH: Is you don't eat before I eat then I eat everything and then I eat you too!

JUDY rises from her chair definitely concerned now

JUDY: I think I'll get the Mistress

PUNCH grabs her arm and eases her into her chair

25. Guzzling sequence. Punch (as Himself) with Judy

PUNCH: You like? (*JUDY nods*) You eat. (*Offers her tureens in turn. JUDY is very nervous*) More? (*JUDY shakes her head*) Good. You sure?
JUDY: Yes.
PUNCH: (*With sudden violence*) Then for ever keep your trap shut mouth!

In seconds, he tilts the table so that all the tureens of food slide to him. He tastes the contents of each tureen in turn then attacks all with abandon – grotesque stuffing

JUDY: Ugh! (*Vomits*)
PUNCH: (*Spitting out bits of food as he speaks*) Something smashing wrong? (*Judy vomits again*) Good. Nothing wrong. (*Back to food*) Smash smash smashingest food I ever had in my whole... smash...
JUDY: (*Becoming suspicious*) Are you sure that you're... ?

Notices slapstick for the first time. Leans over and removes it whilst PUNCH is gorging

I knew it! (*Cracks him on the head*) Knew it! You lying pig! (*Hits him*) You maroon you... get out!
PUNCH: Eh?
JUDY: Out!

PUNCH: Eh Judy!
JUDY: Now!
PUNCH: Listen Judy.
JUDY: You listen! *Out!* (*Hits him*) *Now!*
PUNCH: (*Really staggering this time*) Can't Judy. Can't. I the Master
(*Threatens him again with the slapstick*) No! We swap! *He* gardener now.
He wanted to, so...

*Does a quick mime of the swap, during which JUDY is so amused that she
loses concentration and is duped into giving PUNCH back his slapstick*

so you stop!

Mighty crack on the table. JUDY is terrified

and marry me...!
JUDY: (*Cowering*) What?
PUNCH: (*Grinning*) Marry me... cuddle me an' pudding me an' makes
me lots of babies with me cos I the rich an' Master of money of plenty
everything...! So wadyasay?
JUDY: (*Stunned*) Flipped. I say you flipped. You lying flipped. I say you
get out. Now!
PUNCH: Judy...?
JUDY: Now. Else I fetch the Master.
PUNCH: (*Adopting Himself's attitude*) I the Master.
JUDY: Doesn't bear thinking about. I mean, look at you standing there
dolled up like that. If you think that grabs me then you're even more
stupid than you think I am. Who would 'ave believed it, who would
'ave thought it... on your first day. Well m'lad you've 'ad it. Done, gone,
finish! No woo for you m'lad... (*PUNCH groans*) None of that either.
Don't think you can soft-soap me... (*A different groan*) or that.
PUNCH: Judy...?
JUDY: And you've tried that too often. Marry you, *Me* marry *you*. You
must be a lunatic. You *are* a lunatic! *Me... you? You...* woo *me* ever
again... after this... *you?*
PUNCH: (*Hangdog*) Me. I make you laughs silly Judy most of... I do...
Judy?

Pause. JUDY is caught

JUDY: Give us a kiss.
PUNCH: (*Hideous grin*) No!
JUDY: Go on... (*Embracing him*) Kissy kissy kissy...

They go into a 'catch-a-kiss-if-you're-clever-enough' Lazzo

Whilst thus engaged HIMSELF enters and unobtrusively tries to attract PUNCH'S attention. JUDY conducts an appraisal of PUNCH'S adopted clothes

JUDY: You do look nice though Punchy (*Kisses PUNCH*)
PUNCH: (*Gormless*) Do I?
JUDY: Yeh! (*Kisses Punch*)
Fingering his jacket) Beautiful. Ooo 'a could! (*Kisses PUNCH*)
PUNCH: Yeh!
JUDY: Right now! (*Kisses PUNCH*) 'Ere. (*Kiss*) Now (*Kiss*) In fact... (*Starts to unbutton PUNCH's jacket kissing him as she does it*) I am...!
HIMSELF: Er excuse me! (*Louder*) Excuse me! (*PUNCH notices HIMSELF*)
JUDY: (*Leaping back*) You did that while I was kissing you 'Ow you do it ?

PUNCH notices HIMSELF for the first time. HIMSELF indicates to PUNCH that he continues the 'mouthing'. PUNCH grins in acknowledgment and begins a rhetorical strut ensuring that HIMSELF stays out of JUDY's vision

HIMSELF: (*Laying special emphasis on the accent – e.g. 'sined' for 'sound' with PUNCH 'mouthing'*) We all do it, Have to. Very necessary to know high to talk properly... articulate. To be able to produce a very special sind which is common to all ire sort who come from ire sort of backgrinde. It identifies us. All traces of roughness erased, rubbed light. Consider Nanny's accent. Broad, soft, lush, romantic even. All gone. Removed. Every tiny Nanny sined which we reproduced naturally as children was beaten ite of us at school or laughed ite of us by our peers – or both. (*Musing*) I loved Nanny, especially when she read to me in bed. Loved it. So... warm. I will never be able to sined like that...

JUDY: I never knew you 'ad a Nanny?
PUNCH: (*Normal*) I did I did I did 'ave a Nanny. Fanny. That was it. Fanny Nanny Nanny Fanny.
JUDY: You've changed your voice. 'Ere, what's going on?

HERSELF enters.

HERSELF: That's What I'd like to know.

JUDY instantly begins clearing the table. HERSELF notices HIMSELF as GARDENER

What are *you* doing in *here*?
HIMSELF: Er...?
PUNCH: Problem.
HERSELF: Already?

PUNCH: Yes.
HERSELF: Yes?
PUNCH: Oh Yes.
HERSELF: In here?
PUNCH: Yes here yes.
HERSELF: Why are you still using that stupid voice?
PUNCH: (*Clearing his throat*) Ahhhhhhh, throat very bad. Very very very bad... very.
HERSELF: No need to go on about it. I think you'd better deal with *this* (*Nods to HIMSELF*) and explain to him that in the future, all business relating to the garden is conducted *in* the garden and not, I repeat *not* in *here*! No precedents please.

PUNCH repeats bits of what she says almost as she is saying it, odd juicy words such as 'not presidents' being especially heard. JUDY begins to scuttle out with an armful of tureens

Judy? A word please.
JUDY: Yes miss. (*She changes her course to follow 'HERSELF'*)
HERSELF: You won't be needing those.

JUDY drops the tureens and follows in the wake of 'HERSELF' sniggering unbelievingly at PUNCH and HIMSELF as she does so

SCENE SEVENTEEN – Drawing Room as before. Single Ornate Chair

By the time Herself and JUDY have settled into this next scene, HIMSELF and PUNCH have shuffled unobtrusively to the perimeter.

HERSELF: Something has to be done!
JUDY: Yes.
HERSELF: Sit down!
JUDY: Eh?
HERSELF: Please sit down Judy, it helps me feel positive.
JUDY: You wha?
HERSELF: Please...
JUDY: Right. (*Sits*)
HERSELF: (*Beside herself*) Did you see? Did you?
JUDY: Eh?
HERSELF: See!
JUDY: Oh Yeh. What?

HERSELF: Did you see... *Him*?!

JUDY: (*Pretending to assume she is referring to the gardener... one of her streams of unconciousness*) I know it's cos 'es new when we've got 'im trained 'e'll be as good as gold like me know 'is place jump when 'es asked no 'olding 'im like a frog 'e'll be jump jump jump anyway today's 'is first day bound to make a few mistakes but 'e'll learn 'e'll not come into the kitchen again I'll see to that in the kitchen 'e'll be 'opping about (*Laughs*) like a Frog.

HERSELF: Not!

JUDY: Eh?

HERSELF: Not *him*. The menopausal Master I mean. Did you see what he did at the table. I mean, if his mother knew she'd... well!

JUDY: (*Mock surprise*) Oh... the Master. Well I shouldn't worry too much.

HERSELF: Not?

JUDY: No.

HERSELF: *Not* worry?

JUDY: Course not.

HERSELF: Well I am. In fact Judy I've decided.

JUDY: (*Matter of fact*) Right.

HERSELF: I'm left with no choice.

JUDY: Right.

HERSELF: I'm leaving.

JUDY: (*Bright*) Right...

HERSELF: Tonight...

JUDY: (*Very bright*) Right.

HERSELF: And I need your help.

JUDY: I knew there was a catch in it.

HERSELF: Go through all my things and pack them. Arrange transport, accommodation, all that sort of thing. Understand?

JUDY: Oh yes Miss (*Standing*)

HERSELF: Why are you standing? Sit down.

JUDY: (*Sitting*) I think before you I and me collect you accommodation arrange your things an' all that... there's something you ought to know.

HERSELF: What on earth did I 'ought' to know? I know enough. I experienced it. He *touched* me, *there*. (*Points to the offended spot*) *Never* has he done that before.

JUDY: Never?

HERSELF: Never.

JUDY: What a shame. You poor thing. Well anyway, did you notice anything different about 'im I mean at lunch and after... Anything?

HERSELF: Of course! That's what I've been talking about – why I'm leaving.

JUDY: No. I mean *odd*.

HERSELF: *Odd*? Of course I did I...

JUDY: No!! I mean so odd you couldn't believe it (*HERSELF speechless*) I mean *so odd* it could've been someone else?

HERSELF: You mean he's a schizophrenic?

JUDY: No... ... odd!!!

HERSELF: (*Sudden realisation*) You're right Judy. You're right! There was definitely something...

JUDY: I know.

HERSELF: You do? What do you know?

JUDY: They swapped!

HERSELF: I don't understand.

JUDY: Neither do I but they 'ave. 'E's... 'im and 'im's 'e. Swapped!

HERSELF: You're mad!

JUDY: *They* are! But I did like Punch all dressed up like the Master and when 'e spoke like 'im well I 'ad to admit that I liked it I really did...

HERSELF: You mean to say that the Master, *my* husband, has become metamorphosed into *your* Mr Punch – *our* gardener – and that they have both agreed to this?

JUDY: Agree I'm not sure about, but done it...

HERSELF: Yes?

JUDY: They 'ave. Very clever.

HERSELF gropes for a chair, JUDY stands, HERSELF sits

HERSELF: I feel sick!

JUDY: I can tell.

HERSELF: I can't believe it.

JUDY: Neither can I but there we are...

HERSELF: What am I going to do?

JUDY: (*Quietly evil*) What *I'm* going to do?

HERSELF: Yes, but what am *I* going to do?

JUDY: (*Stronger*) What *I'm* going to do.

HERSELF: Yes?

JUDY: The same.

HERSELF: (*Without comprehending*) Really?

JUDY: (*Evil joy*) *I'm* going to swap with *you.*

HERSELF: I think I'm *going* to be sick!

JUDY: I can tell.

HERSELF: No.

JUDY: Yes.

HERSELF: No.

JUDY: *You* teach *me* 'ow to be *you*...

HERSELF: No!

JUDY: And I'll teach *you* 'ow to be *me.*

HERSELF: No!!
JUDY: In that case... (*Begins to remove apron*)
HERSELF: No!!
JUDY: (*Apron removed*) I'm going!
HERSELF: (*Panic-stricken*) No!!! No Judy don't do that. (*Very melodramatic*) I'll do as you say.
JUDY: Knew you would. But you 'ave to promise one thing.
HERSELF: Anything!
JUDY: We don't tell them.
HERSELF: What?!
JUDY: (*Threatens with apron again*) Or else...
HERSELF: Anything!
JUDY: Knew you would. What a laugh I'm beside yourself. Now this is what we'll do. First of all I'll tell *you* about *me*.

Hands apron to HERSELF

You'll be needing this.

SCENE EIGHTEEN

As JUDY and HERSELF move aside, PUNCH and HIMSELF become activated, HIMSELF teaching PUNCH the essentials of being... 'Himself'.

HIMSELF: The first thing you have to learn is to keep still.

PUNCH shifts about like a child suffering from worms

PUNCH: Yeh.
HIMSELF: Absolutely still.

The more PUNCH tries the worse it becomes

PUNCH: Yeh.
HIMSELF: That's the first thing (*Extraordinary squirm by PUNCH*) Failed!
PUNCH: Yeh (*Almost falls over*)
HIMSELF: Can't progress until you've learned the art of stillness. Stillness is strength!
PUNCH: Stillness is strength. Yeh. Remember, stillness strong.

Develops a quick, grotesque sequence of 'strength' revelations. Gets them all going, then suddenly, absolute stillness

Yeh (*statuesque*) There (*falls like a log*) Got it. Right. Next (*gets eagerly to his feet*) I soon be you. I nearly you already.

HIMSELF: You *are* me. You must never lose sight of that. Just need to refine one or two details to complete the illusion. Can't afford any slip-ups can we? Got to be able to carry it off to the last – well almost the last – detail. So... again? Mmm?
PUNCH: No need. Look. I got it. (*Goes through the same routine again*) Easy (*falls over*) See? Got it. Easy!
HIMSELF: I'm not quite sure you understand.
PUNCH: (*Mock defensive*) What you mean? I still enough isn't I was? I very strong. No one goes for me in a Russian. Smash 'm to bits, rip 'm apart!! (*Instant grin*) Right. Next?
HIMSELF: (*Slightly alarmed*) Well... (*Adopts a philosophising pose*)
PUNCH: (*Watching very closely*) 'Ow you do that?
HIMSELF: Well (*resets pose*) You see... (*Big speech emerging*)
PUNCH: (*Mimicking*) You see...

HIMSELF moves around as he develops his argument

HIMSELF: Strength...
PUNCH: Strength (*Mimicking*) Yeh. Got that... Strength...
HIMSELF: Is not just a matter of being strong.
PUNCH: Yeh. No. Stupid. Yeh Got that...
HIMSELF: Not just...
PUNCH: Not just...
HIMSELF: Physical strength...
PUNCH: 'S'cal strength. Yeh...
HIMSELF: More a matter of emotional strength, an awareness, presence, authority of the *mind, not* muscle...
PUNCH: (*Totally confused*) Yeh. Got that. Yeh.
HIMSELF: That's *one* way.
PUNCH: Got it. Easy. Yeh. Yeh... ?
HIMSELF: The *wrong* way.
PUNCH: Yeh. Got it the wrong way. Easy.
HIMSELF: Try and forget that.
PUNCH: Easy. Gone.
HIMSELF: Let's try it again with a minimum of movement.
PUNCH: You mean keep still?
HIMSELF: Yes.
PUNCH: You mean, not even a twitch?
HIMSELF: Precisely (*PUNCH hasn't a clue*) Yes.

PUNCH adopts a pose of new resolve. Very excited

PUNCH: Ready!

HIMSELF: (*Posing slightly, speaking slowly. Punch watches with increasing tension*) You have to be... balanced, feet carefully placed. Your head still, your hands still, your eyes fixed, relaxed, perfectly relaxed. Voice gentle though persuasive. Every rhetorical device you can possibly think of... especially... (*Pointing the 'rhetorical questions'*) Don't you think?

PUNCH: What?

HIMSELF: Isn't it, aren't you, doesn't he?

PUNCH: Eh?

HIMSELF: And no! Definitely not! Can't be done! You can't be serious?!

PUNCH: Eh?

HIMSELF: (*Relaxing smile*) That sort of thing.

PUNCH: Yeh.

HIMSELF: Rhetoric.

PUNCH: Yeh.

HIMSELF: You try.

PUNCH: Er... (*Grotesque confusion*)

HIMSELF: (*Suddenly*) I think I'll go for a walk.

PUNCH: Eh?

HIMSELF: (*Walking away*) Beautiful day isn't it?

PUNCH: Is it?

HIMSELF: (*Turning. Still*) Lesson *Three*.

PUNCH: (*Becoming angry*) Stop it stop it stop it! I 'aven't tried 'rhetoric' yet, 'ave I?

HIMSELF: (*Smiling*) you've plenty to get on with, haven't you?

PUNCH: Haven't I?

HIMSELF: Haven't you?

PUNCH: Haven't I?

HIMSELF: Haven't you?

PUNCH: (*Very angry*) Haven't I?!!

Suddenly clicks. Perfect mimicry of 'Himself'

PUNCH: Yes. While you in the garden, you find a couple of braces of pheasants in the game store. You will give them a good pluck a – won't you?

HIMSELF: (*Impressed*) You've got it haven't you?

PUNCH: I think so, don't you?

HIMSELF: Amazing isn't it?

PUNCH: I am aren't I (*HIMSELF spins on his heel and begins to walk away*) Where you go?

HIMSELF: (*Stopping*) I'll leave that with you then.

PUNCH: What is you left? I don' unstand all at all... (*Instant grin*) Isn't it?

HIMSELF: (*Slowly. Deliberately*) Ask questions – rhetorical questions that is – then ignore the response completely. Make an excuse, and leave. The best one of all is the 'bollocking' technique. Rarely justified, but produces a wonderful edge to a working relationship between Master and minions. Blast them with displeasure, using all the vein – bulging pique you can muster. Make it long and sound convincingly argued. It has greatest impact when it doesn't make any sense whatsoever. Conclude with a rhetorical question, to which – of course – you have already supplied the answer you require, and then – this is the best bit – say something like, 'I'll leave it with you then'. Spin on your heel and move quickly away before they can reply. Quite shakes them. You can feel the bubbles rising. Work-rate goes up by two hundred percent for a few days, then levels out to a happy 'efficient' for a few weeks, by which time you're looking for the next 'bollocking'... ad infinitum.

So... lesson three is, never listen to any minion's replies, requests, ideas, complaints – anything! Never! (*PUNCH is asleep*)

Lesson four... you're brighter than I thought.

PUNCH: (*Waking*) Eh?

HIMSELF: (*Chuckling*) You really surprised me.

PUNCH: (*With relish*) Gosh!

HIMSELF: Really.

PUNCH: You very good patronising git!

HIMSELF: (*Clapping his hands*) Right. The final touch. *Very* good. End of lesson.

PUNCH: (*Mimicking*)Very good.

HIMSELF: Amazing.

PUNCH: (*Mimicking perfectly now*) Very very very... (*Pause*) good. Now...

HIMSELF: Yes?

PUNCH: (*Being Punch*) Lesson one. You!

HIMSELF: Ah.

PUNCH: You. *You* do *me*!

HIMSELF: You?

PUNCH: Me

Hits HIMSELF on the head with the slapstick

You (*Smack*) silly old coot! (*Smack*) Hit fast! (*Smack*) Hit hard! (*Smack*) Lesson one. Lesson two... (*Smack*)

SCENE NINETEEN

HERSELF and JUDY as before. HERSELF is sitting in the chair bewailing her lot.

HERSELF: I can't Judy. I can't do it.

JUDY: Then you keep the apron. Suits you. (*Walks away*)

HERSELF: Judy please... (*JUDY stops*) I'll do whatever you say. Where shall I start?

JUDY: Now 'Ere. Tell me 'ow to be *you*.

HERSELF: Well...

JUDY: Yes?

HERSELF: Well... The first thing, is to learn how to *do* nothing. Enjoy *nothing*.

JUDY: Eh?

HERSELF: Absolutely nothing! Enjoy it.

JUDY: You mean... No work?

HERSELF: Good god, no *work*! Ugh! Except of course...

JUDY: Yeh?

HERSELF: On yourself.

JUDY: Me?

HERSELF: Your voice, your clothes (*looking at JUDY doubtfully*) your style. You as *you* Judy, fine. *If* you are to become *me* then... lots of work. Very difficult.

JUDY: Why d'you say that? I can do what you do. (*Adopts herself's posture*) 'Ow do I look?

HERSELF: Well, actually...

JUDY: (*Sharp*) I know that one. Watched you do *that* one many times. Not to me. You always tell *me*. But *your* lot, never.

HERSELF: (*Mock naive*) What don't I do Judy?

JUDY: Tel 'em what you feel about anything 'specially if you don't like it.

HERSELF: Well observed Judy. Very good. You're right. Keep them sweet and you'll have sweetness in return. Aim always to flatter. Bluntness is base, beneath, down there. But we're jumping ahead a little. Before all of that, *look* good.

JUDY: I could look good if I'ad your money.

HERSELF: Perhaps... .

JUDY: Liar!

HERSELF: You spotted it. (*Even more patronising*) Good...

JUDY: What you keep saying 'good' for when you don't mean it?

HERSELF: (*Getting quite excited*) Good. You're learning . I agree with you. I think you're a scruffy little ragbag. A smelly, ugly, disgustingly awful woman.

JUDY: (*Brightening. Mimicking*) Thank you. You're very sweet.

Starts copying Herself's attitude

And now, I'd like *you* to listen to *me*.

HERSELF is distinctly perturbed by this, forgetting her new 'subservient' role

HERSELF: Listen to *you*?!
JUDY: You're forgetting yourself my girl. Stop swanning about as though you own the place and listen to what I have to say.
HERSELF: I beg your pardon?
JUDY: When you've finished the pots and prepared dinner, I'd like you to get the gardener to cut some roses. I want to fill the bedroom with roses.
HERSELF: You can't be serious?!
JUDY: (*Stock still*) Very serious. Even more serious than me leaving you if you don't do as you're told! Oh... and I don't want to hear or see '*it*' or shit until further notice.
HERSELF: What?!

JUDY suddenly laughs. Normal

JUDY: I like being you. By the look of you much more than you like being me. Oh yes, one more thing. I'll 'ave that dress you're wearing. Always fancied that dress. And... what's the form in bed you and 'im the Master what's 'e like?
HERSELF: (*Spitting with anger*) Too far! End! Now! Here!
JUDY: (*Equally strong*) No way! I'll find out for myself.
HERSELF: (*Quieter*) There's something I don't think you've quite realised.
JUDY: Go on, spit it out!
HERSELF: If *we* swap, now that *they've* swapped, then we won't, you know, tonight, in bed. We'll remain...
JUDY: Yeh?
HERSELF: As we are, so to speak.
JUDY: Only one thing for it then.
HERSELF: (*Smugly*) What's that?
JUDY: The only way. Stay as we are.
HERSELF: You can't be serious.
JUDY: Am.
HERSELF: Couldn't.
JUDY: No choice.
HERSELF: (*Mock stunned*) Oh! That disgusting, vulgar man!
JUDY: Punch? You talking about Punch? Nothing wrong with Punch. Bright as a button is Punch? Knock spots off the Master.
HERSELF: But he's like an animal.
JUDY: (*Happily*) I know. But 'e learns quick. When you see 'im tonight next to you you won't be able to tell the difference. Well you might but. . .
HERSELF: (*'Herself' once more*) So we're agreed then?

JUDY: Eh?

HERSELF: (*Gently*) To stay as we are.

JUDY: (*Confused*) But we know that they've swapped.

HERSELF: Precisely. *We* know. (*Putting her arm around JUDY*) *Our* secret.

JUDY: (*Duped. Excited*) Yeh. Right.

HERSELF: Just one thing. To *keep* the secret (*Removes apron*) *you'll* need these. (*BABY starts crying off*)

JUDY: Eh? (*Takes apron and puts it on automatically*) Right. Thanks.

HERSELF: Dinner at seven-thirty?

JUDY: Yes Miss.

HERSELF: And please see to *it* will you? I feel exhausted. Think I'll rest for an hour or two. I need to think.

JUDY: (*Totally confused*) Yes Miss. So do I.

SCENE TWENTY – Herself's Bedroom

PUNCH sits fully dressed on the edge of the bed, emptying a box of chocolates and drinking a goblet of wine.

PUNCH: What a day, what a day. Oh dear oh dear oh dear. Best day of my life – since yesterday. Every day just the same. Begins... (*Slumps forward, bored*) ends... (*Quick round of goodies*) What a day! Not finished yet. Best bit left. Me, and the Mistress. (*Crosses his legs over his slapstick. Very painful*) Ahhhhh! Oh dear oh dear oh dear! (*HERSELF enters*)

HERSELF: Aha! There you are.

PUNCH: (*Trying to conceal both the slapstick and the pain*)Yeh... s.

HERSELF: So?

PUNCH: (*Very precise*) So?

HERSELF: So?!

PUNCH: So?!

HERSELF: Stop saying 'so'.

PUNCH: Why?

HERSELF: Because I say so.

PUNCH: Oh. (*Pause*) So?

HERSELF: (*Sighing*) I see. Going to be one of *those* moments is it?

PUNCH: (*Very excited*) Yeh... s!

HERSELF: Before we begin, why are you here?

PUNCH: Tired. I very tired. (*Huge grotesque grin*)

HERSELF: Be that as it may, but why – I repeat – *why* are *you*, *here*?

PUNCH: Here?

HERSELF: Yes.

PUNCH: Here... ?

HERSELF: Here.

PUNCH: Tired.

HERSELF: Yes?
PUNCH: Bed.
HERSELF: Yes?
PUNCH: (*Without thinking uses his slapstick as an indicator*)
    This, bed. You...

Obscene suggestion with slapstick

    Me.

HERSELF: (*Sighing*) I see. I see you on *my* bed. *Your* bed is next door
    where it has always been. (*Points to slapstick*) What's that?
PUNCH: Wand. Magic.
HERSELF: Don't be absurd!
PUNCH: No... magic wand. Put people to sleep. (*Tries a bit of rhetoric*) Put
    you to sleep. Make you happy don't you think?
HERSELF: I don't think.

*She comes closer to PUNCH who lets his 'himself' attitude slip and sits on
the bed stupidly, slapstick dangling*

HERSELF: Look... darling?
PUNCH: (*Beside HIMSELF*) Yeh?
HERSELF: (*Closer*) We've been through all this before, many times.
PUNCH: Have we? Oh yes...
HERSELF: (*Touching PUNCH gently on the shoulder*) Course we have
    darling. You know how you... *sweat* darling?
PUNCH: *Sweat*, darling?
HERSELF: *You* darling. Always *sweat* when you're excited. That's why
    we agreed...
PUNCH: Yeh?
HERSELF: Separate beds, separate rooms.
PUNCH: Keep dry.
HERSELF: Quite.
PUNCH: Quite

PUNCH suddenly grabs HERSELF and soaks her in a quick flurry of kisses

    Kissy kissy kissy (*Stops. Looks up*) Wet kissy! (*Dives in for more*)
HERSELF: (*Struggling desperately*) No... !!
PUNCH: Yeh!
HERSELF: No!! (*Breaks free*) Definitely not!!
PUNCH: (*Huge grin*) Definitely yes!
HERSELF: What's the matter with you today you filthy moron.
PUNCH: You want moron, I moron. Me very dirty moron. Me... anything
    you want.

With much clucking and strutting he chases 'HERSELF' around the room

Kissy kissy kissy.
HERSELF: Moron!
PUNCH: Quack!

HERSELF stamps on PUNCH'S instep which stops his idiocy for a moment

HERSELF: You are a moron, and an idiot. We agreed. *You* in *there, me* in *here*. When I want *you*, I come to *you*. Until that happens, *you* remain in *there*, and *never* but *never* come in *here*. *Ever*!!!
PUNCH: (*Pause. Mock pathetic*) Quack.
HERSELF: So... *go*! Understand?!
PUNCH: Quack.
HERSELF: *Now*!
PUNCH: Quack.

PUNCH suddenly breaks into a spectacular gymnastic routine. Wherever HERSELF turns PUNCH seems to be there blocking her way. He chunters all the time

If you over there, I over here but I come over there so here I come over there and you stay still so I can give you smash smash smashy kissy wissy all over there all over you. Yes please oh yes yes yes! etc...

Finally PUNCH ends up making an acrobatic exit. As he lands he stands still banging and crashing as though he has had a disastrous fall and begins groaning. This is all visible to the audience. He sees HERSELF sit on the edge of the bed with a look of relief. He creeps towards her, groaning and ready to leap on her, but he can't help corpsing in between groans. HERSELF spots this, screams, and runs off with PUNCH in pursuit.

SCENE TWENTY-ONE – Judy's Bedroom

She sits in front of her mirror talking to her snarling reflection.

JUDY: Poxy woman! Thinks she's clever, clever snot! All those pots, all those sausages, all that washing – and '*it*'! All day all night. Never stopped it 'asn't. Tonight, *tonight* Punch and me was going to make a baby. And where is 'e? With 'er that's where 'e is. Thinks she's clever. Well she's no match for Punch. Chase anything 'e will; think nothing of it 'e won't. Make a baby for 'er if 'e gets 'alf a chance 'e will. Make another '*it*'! Can't believe it. (*She is startled by a gentle knock at the door*) Oozat? (*Another knock*) Oo is it?

HIMSELF: (*Trying to mimic Punch*) Me
JUDY: Ooo's me?
HIMSELF: Me.
JUDY: (*Very excited*) Punch! What you doing 'ere? (*Frantic instant powder-ing and make-up session*) 'Ang on! (*Final check. To self*) Right. Right Mr. Bleeding Punch. (*Picks up a play-block as a weapon*) See what you got to say for yourself. (*Stands by the 'door' with the weapon raised*) Come on then Punchy.

HIMSELF enters slowly. JUDY in her eagerness drops the 'weapon' too soon missing HIMSELF by a whisker whilst in his state of shock she grabs his hair and hauls him into the room

Think you're clever don't you? Think you're so clever. Well you're not!

Delivers a terrible blow which sends him sprawling. JUDY then proceeds to systematically work HIMSELF over. This becomes a 'rag doll' Lazzo. When she has finished she stands before his crumpled form

Well? (*Himself groans*) That all you 'ave to say? (*Another groan*) I see...

JUDY prepares for 'round two'

JUDY: Ready for some more? (*HIMSELF tries to crawl away but fails pathetically*) Come on Punch, come and 'ave a fight. (*No response*) Come on Punchy I wanna fight. You know I like a good fight and I've got plenty of fight tonight Punchy. (*Takes a closer look and kneels across his chest*) Punch? (*Tweaks his nose*) Punch?

No response. HIMSELF has a look of death about him

Right

Gets up and makes elaborate 'preparations'

If that's the way, then that's the way. If that's it, then that's it. You want pain – *real* pain – then *real* pain is what you gets: special!

HIMSELF has become spread-eagled at the end of a table. It becomes obvious that JUDY intends to jump from the table onto HIMSELF and inflict her 'special'

This is it. The big one. The big... jump! If you think you can come in 'ere as floppy as a Pheasant and think you can get away with it then you're more stupid than I think I am and you're going to get it good, now! Ready?

She leaps onto the table and measures the distance and area on which she is going to inflict her terrible revenge

A-one, a-two, a...

HIMSELF moves, and in his prone position tries in vain to remove his disguise. JUDY realises that all is not quite right in mid jump and avoids the horrible damage intended by landing with her legs astride HIMSELF'S chest. She peers down at his face for a closer look and realises that all is not well

It's *not* Punch, it's... the Master

Instant physical and verbal summary of the bargain struck earlier with PUNCH, then screams

Better make sure. (*Peers down the front of his trousers*) Ahhhhhh!

'Mad panic' Lazzo begins. Oh shit!
   Goes out and brings on a bucket and mop. Decides against using it, takes it out and comes back with a towel. Unfolds it revealing a hole big enough to tie around the master's neck so that he looks like a child with a bib. Sits him up, lifts him onto her knee, drops him as she reaches for a bottle and decides against it, sits him on her knee again and begins cradling him and cooing, bit like a puppeteer and dummy, very grotesque

Oh... dear. Oh dear oh dear oh dear oh dear oh dear. There there, there there. OOoo's a lovely Master then? OOOooo's a lovely Master Punchy wunchy then...

HIMSELF: (*Just audible*) Hello Judy.
JUDY: Ah my little Punchy.
HIMSELF: Brought you something.
JUDY: Ahhh. 'As me little Master Punchy bought 'is lovely Judy something?
HIMSELF: Yes.
JUDY: An' what's you brought then?
HIMSELF: (*Produces a crumpled rose*) This.

JUDY releases HIMSELF who falls like a log as she concentrates upon the rose

JUDY: Well... look at that just look at that.

Lifts HIMSELF back into a cradling position

You lovely man. I never thought you 'ad it in you. Give us a kiss! (*Sets him up for one*)
HIMSELF: Don't think I can.

JUDY: Course you can. Ready? (*Takes aim*)
HIMSELF: Think so.
JUDY: Steady ...
HIMSELF: (*Very rocky*) Steady...
JUDY: Kissy!

Misses him as he rocks forward. Small 'kiss and miss' Lazzo. JUDY fails to plant a kiss

Only one thing for it.
HIMSELF: Yes?
JUDY: 'Ave to fix you.
HIMSELF: Really?
JUDY: *Really* fix you.
HIMSELF: (*Very doubtful*) Oh...
JUDY: Over 'ere (*Supports himself to the bed*) Now then. (*Stretches him out like a corpse*) That's better. Can't move now. Kiss you now. (*Himself groans*) So... Master Punch, you 'ave brought me a Rose and for that you shall 'ave a 'uge, fat, wetsy, kissy. Ready? (*Himself groans and his head flops to one side*) Oh dear, got the flops 'ave we? Soon fix that. (*Sets his head*) Right. Fixed. (*Takes aim*) Ready?

Final groan before he becomes corpse-like. JUDY springs and envelopes him in a huge, sprawling smacker. She leaps back startled

'Ang on

Puts her hands round his throat and then listens to his chest

'Ang on. I think 'e's dead. The Master, dead! Gone! (*Leaps off the bed*) Fluffed it! Out like a light. Coughed 'is lot 'ere, in *my* bed! I've killed 'im. 'Elp! 'Elp!

New 'panic' Lazzo before returning to HIMSELF checking the pulse of both hands at once

Ahhhhhhhh... !!

Another 'panic' Lazzo

SCENE TWENTY-TWO – (*Continuing*)

Enter HERSELF

JUDY: Ahhhhhhhh!!!!

HERSELF: Judy. Thank God I've found you. Save me from that animal Judy, you can have him!!
JUDY: Can't. 'E's dead!

Goes into a 'clinging, non-releasing' Lazzo. A bit like a fly on gluepaper. As soon as one limb is prised off by HERSELF another becomes stuck – and so on. All the time JUDY is going over a reconstruction of the last scene in one long torrent of gibberish. Lots of variants of 'what are you talking about? And will you get off me' responses from HERSELF to JUDY'S story

HERSELF: Will you keep still?! (*Quick flurry from JUDY, then still*)
JUDY: I couldn't 'elp it.
HERSELF: What *are* you talking about?
JUDY: I was just giving 'im one...
HERSELF: Really?
JUDY: There 'e was right as rain...
HERSELF: Really?
JUDY: On the bed...
HERSELF: Really?!
JUDY: Stretched out, waiting...
HERSELF: I see.
JUDY: There I was, taking aim...
HERSELF: I don't see...
JUDY: Going to do it... !
HERSELF: (*Without a clue as to what JUDY is talking about*) And?
JUDY: Did it.
HERSELF: It?
JUDY: Give 'im one!
HERSELF: And?
JUDY: Coughed 'is lot.
HERSELF: What?!
JUDY: Gone!
HERSELF: He's still there!
JUDY: No! Gone! Out! Dead!
HERSELF: (*Breaking free at last*) Can't be.
JUDY: Is.
HERSELF: Impossible!
JUDY: True!
HERSELF: You must have told him.
JUDY: Never!
HERSELF: Well I didn't.
JUDY: Gone!!

HERSELF goes across to HIMSELF and begins shaking him

HERSELF: We'll soon see about that. Now come along darling its no good, you can't fool me. (*No response*)

JUDY: (*Frightened*) Shouldn't do that.

HERSELF: Why ever not?

JUDY: You'll break things. When they're like that, they snap easy. Not right. Leave 'im in one piece.

HERSELF: Him?! He's done this countless times before. Oldest trick in his tiny mind Judy. Whenever he's challenged, confronted with anything that causes the slightest wobble, out like a light. He plays dead. (*Sits beside him stroking his head*) And I have to play mummy, don't I darling? (*As to a tiny child*) You may *want* to be a gardener darling but you're not going to be a gardener are you darling? (*HIMSELF groans*)

JUDY: OOooer !

HERSELF: You're the Master aren't you darling?

HIMSELF: (*Weakly*) Yes darling.

JUDY: 'E's *not* dead!

HERSELF: Course you're not dead are you darling? Been a difficult day hasn't it darling? Everything's allright now. *I'm* here. (*Lifts him to a sitting position*) There. Feeling better now darling?

HIMSELF: Feel a bit queasy.

HERSELF: Well never mind. Safe now. Soon be better. Couple of weeks in bed and you'll be you old self. There there, soon be better...

The sound of PUNCH's slapstick can be heard, approaching.

PUNCH: (*Calling softly*) Missy. Missy missy. Where are you? Come to Punchy. (*Enters*) Punchy going to kissy missy.

HERSELF: Don't let that idiot come anywhere near me Judy!

PUNCH: Aha!

JUDY: Punch!

PUNCH: I *not* Punch, I the Master. Isn't it?

HERSELF: Idiot!

PUNCH: (*With incredible precision*) No. Me *not* idiot, isn't it. Me Master... won't you (*chuckles to himself*)?

HERSELF: By any stretch of the imagination you are an idiot and you're definitely *not* the Master!

PUNCH: Am!

HERSELF: *Not!* The Master is *here* aren't you darling?

PUNCH: That's not the Master darling aren't you? (*Moves closer to her*) That's Punch the new gardener... won't it?

HERSELF: Don't come any closer!

PUNCH: (*Getting closer*) Yes.

HERSELF: One more step and I'll not be responsible.

PUNCH: (*Very close*) Yes. Won't you?

JUDY: One step closer and I *will* be responsible!
PUNCH: (*Double take*) Ye... who said that?
JUDY: Me.
PUNCH: Who's me?
JUDY: Judy.
PUNCH: Judy?
JUDY: Me.
PUNCH: (*Seeing JUDY for the first time*) Judy! Why didn't you say?
JUDY: Because. Anyway it's all over. We know. Mistress and me you and
　　the Master. We know, finish!
PUNCH: You know, finish?
JUDY: Yes.
PUNCH: (*Pause before mock sorrow*) Oh no!
JUDY: Oh yes.
HERSELF: Oh definitely yes. End. Now!
PUNCH: You mean... (*Mass of meaningless gestures to everyone*)
JUDY: Yes.
PUNCH: Oh no... You mean not even ever never won't you?

HERSELF and JUDY shake their heads.

　What am I going to do?
HERSELF: I'll tell you.
PUNCH: (*Silly*) Yes?
HERSELF: Go!!
PUNCH: Go. Yes.
HERSELF: Now!!

PUNCH moves to exit still very silly

PUNCH: Go, now, yes go...
HERSELF: Haven't you forgotten something?
PUNCH: (*Very silly*) Oh yes!

Goes to MISTRESS and takes her hand to kiss it

HERSELF: Not me you fool! (*Withdrawing her hand in disgust*)
PUNCH: (*Mimicking*) You not me you fool, you *you*!!
HERSELF: (*Unmoved*) Clothes!
PUNCH: (*Very still*) Ye... s?
HERSELF: Give the Master his clothes.
PUNCH: (*Suddenly beginning to remove his clothes*) I take off his clothes...
JUDY: (*Gleefully*) OOooer!
HERSELF: Not here, outside!
PUNCH: Can't.

HERSELF: Why?
PUNCH: He got *my* clothes. Punch has got Master's clothes, and Master...
and Master got Punch's clothes. We swap!
HERSELF: I see. In that case Judy, I think we ought to have a word don't
you? Let them get on with it.

Turns away from them leading a reluctant JUDY with her

SCENE TWENTY-THREE – *A 'changing clothes' Lazzo*

PUNCH: I take off Master's clothes...
HIMSELF: I take off your clothes...
PUNCH: If I take off Master's clothes and you take off my clothes, *we*
take off *my* clothes... I Master, you Punch.
HIMSELF: I don't understand.
PUNCH: You have two clothes, me have none. Me chilly!
HIMSELF: No... I give you my clothes and you give me yours.
PUNCH: I *wearing* your clothes. How you give them to me when I
wearing them?
HIMSELF: No... The clothes you are wearing are *my* clothes. The clothes
I am wearing are your clothes.
PUNCH: Why are you wearing my clothes?
HIMSELF: You gave them to me.
PUNCH: Did I? Very kind.
HIMSELF: I gave mine to you.
PUNCH: Oh. We *both* very kind. (*Gives MASTER a big hug*) What you
think of this? (*Indicates coat he is wearing*)
HIMSELF: (*Realising that this is the only way to solve the problem*) Very
smart.
PUNCH: (*Gesture of great magnanimity*) You can have it. (*Gives him jacket*)
HIMSELF: Very kind. And this? (*Indicates jacket he is wearing*)
PUNCH: Very pretty.
HIMSELF: You can have it. (*They exchange jackets*)
PUNCH: Very kind. (*Points to trousers he is wearing*) These?
HIMSELF: Yes.
PUNCH: Yours. (*MASTER indicates trousers he is wearing*) Yes?
BOTH: *Yours!*

Exchange rest of the clothing and footwear and then embrace

HIMSELF: There.
PUNCH: Where?
HIMSELF: Done.

PUNCH: (*Sniffing the air*) Where?
HIMSELF: As before.
PUNCH: (*Excited*) We swap?
HIMSELF: Yes.
PUNCH: (*Removing his jacket*) Yeh!
HIMSELF: No. We've done that.
PUNCH: (*Suspiciously*) Have we?
HIMSELF: Yes.
PUNCH: (*PUNCH suddenly wields his slapstick menacingly*) I got the job?!
HIMSELF: (*Terrified*) Of course.

They embrace

SCENE TWENTY-FOUR – (*Continuing*)

JUDY and HERSELF

HERSELF: Well we seem to have sorted that out very satisfactorily Judy?
JUDY: Yes Miss.
HERSELF: Been quite an exhausting day.
JUDY: Yes Miss.
HERSELF: I suppose we have to try these things don't we?
JUDY: Yes Miss.
HERSELF: So now we can get back to normal can't we?
JUDY: Yes Miss.
HERSELF: You won't be marrying him will you Judy?
JUDY: Yes Miss.
HERSELF: (*Visibly shaken*) You will?
JUDY: Oh yes Miss. Wherever 'e goes, I go. I love 'im.
HERSELF: You do?
JUDY: Yes Miss.
HERSELF: In that case...
JUDY: Yes miss? (*Begins untying her apron*)
HERSELF: (*Double take*) I hope you're very happy.
JUDY: (*Re-tying apron*) Thank you Miss.
HERSELF: I think it best if he lives *with* you, don't you Judy?
JUDY: I think so Miss.
HERSELF: However, he won't be er... *working* of course will he? We
    couldn't afford him if he were... *working*.
JUDY: Shouldn't think so Miss.
HERSELF: Good. But you will er continue as erm ... ?
JUDY: Oh yes Miss. Thank you Miss (*Embraces her, HERSELF both relieved
    and nauseated*)

SCENE TWENTY-FIVE – (*Continuing*)

HIMSELF and PUNCH join the two women.

HIMSELF: (*Fully recovered*) Darling?
HERSELF: Yes darling?
HIMSELF: Darling erm... Mr Punch has agreed happily to become our new gardener.
HERSELF: Oh I am glad. Just one thing darling... .
HIMSELF: Yes darling?
HERSELF: He won't *do* anything will he darling?
HIMSELF: Good Lord no. Not a thing darling.
HERSELF: That's settled then.

An 'introductions' Lazzo develops

HIMSELF: (*Introducing*) Meet erm...
PUNCH: (*Mock shy*) Hello.
HERSELF: Hello (*Stops short of actually shaking his hand*)
PUNCH: Hello.
HIMSELF: (*Introducing*) Judy...
JUDY: Hello (*shake hands*)
PUNCH: Hello

Pause.

HIMSELF: And me...
PUNCH: (*Very mock shy*) Hello.
JUDY: (*Cheekily*) 'E won't be doing anything will 'e?
HERSELF: Good Lord no!
HIMSELF: Definitely not!

PUNCH looks for another round this time with PUNCH in charge of introductions

PUNCH: Er...

Indicates HERSELF but she declines impatiently this time

Hello..

HIMSELF: Hello.
PUNCH: Judy? (*JUDY offers hand giggling*)
HIMSELF: Hello. (*Shakes hand*)
PUNCH: And me... gardener darling, isn't it? (*Bursts into laughter*)
HIMSELF: Hello. (*Shakes hand*)

Pause.

HERSELF: Well?
PUNCH: Well? (*continues saying this*)
JUDY: Well?
HIMSELF: Well?
HERSELF: I think so darling. Yes. Tonight. I think so. You've been *very* good...
HIMSELF: (*Double take*) Thank *you* darling.
HERSELF: Shall we? (*Indicates to go*)
HIMSELF: (*Excited*) Think so.
HERSELF: Goodnight. See you tomorrow.
HIMSELF: Afternoon (*Quiet chuckle*)

HERSELF and HIMSELF have the following exchange as they walk off.

HERSELF: Did I catch something untoward in your tone darling?
HIMSELF: Don't think so darling.
HERSELF: An... inference. You seemed rather excited about something.
HIMSELF: I am!
HERSELF: That's what I thought...

SCENE TWENTY-SIX

As HIMSELF and HERSELF exit so Judy's bedroom is established.
JUDY is 'making up' and grinning hideously, PUNCH is watching her even more hideous swinging his slapstick.

PUNCH: Dooty dooty doo, dooty dooty dooty ... (*Pause*) Judy?
JUDY: (*Applying more make up*) Yes?
PUNCH: Judy?
JUDY: Just a minute!
PUNCH: Judy?!
JUDY: Yes?!
PUNCH: Can I hit you?
JUDY: In a minute!
PUNCH: (*Sloppily*) Can I bash you an' smash you an' belt you an' bite you an' rip your ears off an' push your nose in an' crush your instep... can I?
JUDY: (*Gently*) Course you can.
PUNCH: 'S allright then (*Starts to get up*)
JUDY: In a minute.
PUNCH: O.K. (*Sits down*)

Pause

out of mask   in mask.

26. Out of and in mask

Eh Judy? Before I do that Judy, before I bash you an' smash you an' rip you to bits... can I woo you?
JUDY: (*Finished. Final check*) Oh I should think so...
PUNCH: Yeh?

Judy moves coyly towards him. Extraordinarily grotesque

JUDY: If you want to...
PUNCH: (*Puzzling thought coming on*) Eh Judy?
JUDY: (*Displayed before him now*) Yes?
PUNCH: (*Thought becoming a problem*) Judy?
JUDY: Yes?
PUNCH: (*Snapping slapstick*) Judy?!!
JUDY: (*Very excited*) Yes?!!!
PUNCH: How you do *it*?

Absolute stillness for say three seconds. Suddenly the baby squawls in the distance. Judy puts on her apron, goes out, and returns snatching the slapstick from the bemused Punch.

JUDY: I dunno. Better ask 'it' (*And whacks him with the slapstick*)
'Crying curtain' Lazzo or the 'curtain crying' Lazzo – whichever way you want to do it!

DAVID GRIFFITHS

JUDY goes to HIMSELF and HERSELF in turn, whacks them with the slapstick. They begin crying and line up crying beside PUNCH, who after much gawping at the crying pair eventually starts crying with them. JUDY returns and PUNCH goes through a ridiculous mime of how the crying started and manoeuvres the slapstick into his hands and whacks JUDY so that she starts crying and everyone else cries louder.

They are in a line facing the audience and remain crying for the first curtain and stop when they remove their masks.

End

100

APPENDIX

Making a leather mask

I don't intend to describe all the technicalities of design, moulding and caving a wooden matrix. These are skills which belong to the sculptor and mask carver and sometimes take years to learn. Forming a leather mask on the matrix however is not too difficult and so I shall describe this part of the process in more detail.

MATRIX: Once the design of the mask has been established and the dimensions of the face of the wearer recorded then the character is modelled in clay, a cast made in plaster, and templates cut in card of cross-sections of the outer moulding of the features.

From these templates a matrix is carved out of woods such as gelutong, lime or cypress (see 'The Noh Mask' in Volume 2), remembering to allow for the additional thickness of the leather in the measurements.

Because the leather is wet when it is worked over the matrix it is important to seal the wood by covering it in coats of varnish to make it water-resistant.

WORKING THE LEATHER: The leather needs to be a natural skin which has been tanned using a vegetable process. This makes it easier to work with. The more detailed the features on the mask the thinner the

27. Making a leather mask

skin, but there is a limit to which a thin skin can retain its rigid moulded shape. I would never make a mask in leather less than 1mm thick.

The leather is cut so that it will comfortably cover the matrix – allowing for the extra three-dimensional element of the moulding – and then left immersed in cold water for a couple of hours or so.

This is then drained, pushed into the moulded features, secured to the outer edge of the matrix with brass pins, and tapped into the surface using an assortment of mallets and fine, bone, forming tools. This process takes time, skill and patience developing the forming of the leather by chasing the folds to the edges, and gently crushing the leather – a bit like 'beating' copper.

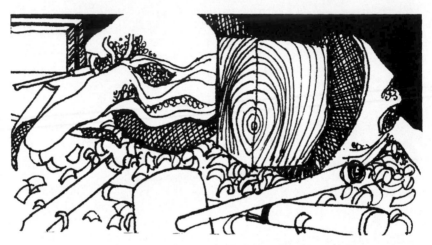

28. Making a leather mask. Carve the mask relief

29. Attaching the soaked leather onto the mould

30. Cutting the mask from the mould

Where the features leap off the face, like – for example – the exaggerated nose of Capitano, then the folds which often gather around the nose have to be flattened, bits cut out, flaps created and folded over each other in the re-joining process.

Once the leather has been carefully beaten over the contours of the matrix, then the eye holes are cut as well as the residue of leather outside the retaining brass pins which secure the leather to the matrix. Allow to dry and remove.

The perimeter of the back of the mask can be stiffened by covering a measured length of thin wire with the shaved flaps of excess leather. It is better if these flaps are thinned down so that they become more flexible to stick over the wire. Use an impact adhesive for this and to join the flaps formed in the mask where folds have been cut and removed. All the time this is being done keep replacing the mask over the matrix to check that distortion is not taking place. In any case it is useful to have the wooden form underneath the leather to enable the flaps to be firmed down.

COLOURING: Paint cracks and peels away from a 'living' surface like leather so it is preferable in the long term to use aniline dyes to colour the surface. A rag ball is as good as anything to apply the dye, with the fine detail being left for the brush.

Dark tones tend to eliminate the three-dimensional aspect of the mask design as they absorb light. The dye should be applied in thinned, even coats of light tones, and continually tested in something resembling the performance light until the required tone is achieved. Try to avoid 'blotting' with excess dye by wiping and thus testing the application on a rejected bit of leather or newspaper.

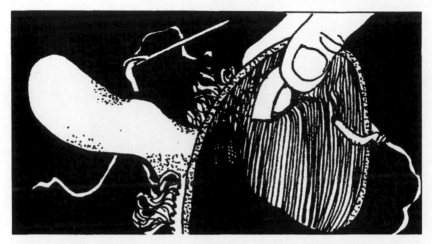

31. Stitching the eyebrows and covering inside with tape

Finally eyebrows and hair can be added by stitching material through appropriately punched holes and tying off on the inside, covering the knots and loose ends with tape or bits of shaved leather; a bit like the method used to make a wig.

If you would like further details of where to attend courses to make leather masks then I suggest you contact the Scottish Mask and Puppet Centre in Glasgow.

INDEX